Living the Jubilee

Other Books of Interest from St. Augustine's Press

George Gänswein with Saverio Gaeta, *Who Believes Is Not Alone: My Life Beside Benedict XVI*

Saverio Gaeta, *Living Medjugorje*

Donald S. Prudlo and Paul J. Voss, *Merchant Saint: The Church, the Market, and the First Lay Canonization*

Donald S. Prudlo, *Governing Perfection*

Bartholemew of the Martyrs, O.P., (Donald S. Prudlo translator), *Stimulus Pastorum: A Charge to Pastors*

Ralph McInerny, *Defamation of Pius XII*

Peter Kreeft, *I Surf, Therefore I Am: A Philosophy of Surfing*

Peter Kreeft, *Socratic Logic 3.1e: Socratic Method Platonic Questions*

Peter Kreeft, *Ha!: A Christian Philosophy of Humor*

Peter Kreeft, *The Philosophy of Jesus*

Gerard V. Bradley, *Unquiet Americans: U.S. Catholics, Moral Truth, and the Preservation of Civil Liberties*

Gerard V. Bradley, *Essays on Law, Religion, and Morality*

Adrian Reimers, *The Ethos of the Christian Heart: Reading Veritatis Splendor*

M. Pascalina Lehnert and Susan Johnson, *His Humble Servant: Sister M. Pascalina Lehnert's Memoirs of Her Years of Service to Eugenio Pacelli, Pope Pius XII*

Giulio Maspero, After Pandemic, *After Modernity: The Relational Revolution*

Francisco Insa, *The Formation of Affectivity: A Christian Approach*

James V. Schall, *At a Breezy Time of Day: Selected Schall Interviews on Just about Everything*

Catherine Godfrey-Howell, *Consensual Incapacity to Marry*

Living the Jubilee
Saverio Gaeta

St. Augustine's Press
South Bend, Indiana

VIVERE IL GIUBILEO
by Saverio Gaeta
© 2024 Mondadori Libri S.p.A.
Published by Mondadori under the imprint of Piemme

Manufactured in the United States of America.

1 2 3 4 5 6 30 29 28 27 26 25

Library of Congress Control Number: 2025932176

Paperback ISBN: 978-1-58731-458-2
Ebook ISBN: 978-1-58731-463-6

∞ The paper used in this publication meets the minimum requirements of the American National Standard for Information Sciences – Permanence of Paper for Printed Materials, ANSI Z39.48-1984.

St. Augustine's Press
www.staugustine.net

Cover image by Anastassia Cassady, watercolor entitled *Saint Peter's Vigil*

TABLE OF CONTENTS

INTRODUCTION

The 30th Jubilee of historical record will take place from December 24, 2024, to January 6, 2026, and Pope Francis has proclaimed this a time to solemnize the birth of Jesus Christ, in accordance with the now customary 25-year cycle of such celebrations. This follows in close continuity with the Ordinary Holy Year of 2000, during which John Paul II strongly invited all of humanity to enter the Third Millennium in the light of Christian hope; it is also connected to the Extraordinary Holy Year of 2015, to which Pope Francis committed the task of reintroducing a world in crisis to the infinite mercy of God.

The pope has chosen to merge the themes of hope and mercy as a key to interpreting the human adventure, with particular attention given to our challenging times that are fraught with anxiety. Yet even in our day faith still has something important to say and urges all to open their hearts to trust in the loving presence of God who guides the steps of men and women throughout all of history toward a destiny filled with goodness.

Indeed, the Jubilee has its very roots in the dawn of the covenant between the Creator and the chosen people, decisively sealed upon the endowment of the tablets of the Law to Moses on Mount Sinai around 1250 BC. Just forty years later, in 1207 BC, the first celebration took place, following the norms codified by God in Leviticus 25: "You shall count seven weeks of years, seven times seven years; these seven weeks of years shall make forty-nine years. Then, on the tenth day of the seventh month, you shall sound the trumpet; on the Day of Atonement you shall sound the trumpet throughout the land. You shall sanctify the fiftieth year, and proclaim liberty throughout the land for all its inhabitants."

A ram's horn was used to signal the start of the celebration, in Hebrew called *qéren jôbél* (from which the term "Jubilee" is derived). This instrument was used in particular moments in Israel's history: "Only when the ram's horn sounds may they go up the mountain" (Exodus 19:13); These are, for example, God's words to Moses on Mount Sinai. The same sound echoed during the taking of Jericho: "When the ram's horn sounds, as soon as you hear the trumpet, the whole people shall shout with a great shout, then the walls of the city will fall down, and the people will go up, each one straight ahead" (Joshua 6:5–6).

Relating to the spiritual dimension, the Jewish Jubilee also possessed a social dimension, for it was decreed that in such a year all would regain ownership of previously sold properties with a "bare ownership" *ante litteram*: "You shall regulate the purchase from your neighbor based on the number of years since the last Jubilee: he will sell to you based on the years of harvest. The more years remain, the more you will increase the price; the fewer years remain, the more you will reduce the price, for he is selling to you the number of harvests." However, historians largely agree that such a radical form of restitution was not the norm, but stood as a kind of ideal guideline maintained to combat injustice.

Jesus Himself engaged with this tradition when He read a biblical passage in the synagogue of Nazareth: "The Spirit of the Lord is upon me; for this reason, He has anointed me and sent me to bring good news to the poor, to proclaim release to the captives and recovery of sight to the blind; to set free the oppressed, to proclaim the year of the Lord's favor" (Isaiah 61:1–2). And He explained it in this way: "Today this Scripture has been fulfilled in your hearing" (Luke 4:21).

At the end of the 4th century, Saint Jerome in his complete Latin translation of the Bible coined the word *iubilaeus*, linking it also to the notion of joy. This concept was later elaborated by medieval theologians and eventually promulgated within the papal bull issued announcing the Fifth Crusade in 1217: "A favorable time is near, and the day of salvation is coming, for those who have sold themselves to the devil for the price of their sins shall recover their lost freedom in the joy of the new Jubilee."

In fact, even as the first Holy Year of 1300 was yet quite distant in the horizon, the "paths of grace," as Pope Francis called them, had already been marked whereby divine mercy abundantly poured out upon the people of God. As early as 992, Pope John XV had instituted the Jubilee at the French shrine of Le Puy-en-Velay, to be celebrated every time the liturgy of March 25 commemorated both the conception of Jesus (the Annunciation) and His death on the cross (Good Friday). (The last occurrence of this convergence was in 2016, and the next will not happen until 2157.) In 1216, Pope Honorius III granted St. Francis of Assisi's request for an indulgence for those who visited the Porziuncola on the first two days of August. A few years later, in 1122, Pope Callixtus II granted the celebration of the Jubilee at the shrine of Santiago de Compostela every time July 25, the feast of the Apostle James, fell on a Sunday. In 1294, Pope Celestine V established the "perdonanza" (forgiveness) for pilgrims at the Basilica of Santa Maria di Collemaggio in Aquila on August 28–29 each year.

These are all circumstances, as Pope Francis reminds us, that emphasize "how the Christian life is a journey that also needs significant moments to nurture and strengthen hope, an indispensable companion that allows us to glimpse the ultimate goal: the encounter with the Lord Jesus." It is therefore "good that this 'widespread' modality of Jubilee celebrations continues, so that the power of God's forgiveness sustains and accompanies the journey of communities and individuals." This is the pope's encouragement of how we are to live this Holy Year well, exhorting "pilgrims of hope" to "set out in search of the meaning of life and to rediscover the value of silence, effort in hardship, and simplicity."

1
THE JUBILEE OF HOPE

A Light in the Difficult Present

A time to "rekindle hope": One might summarize the meaning and purpose of the Holy Year 2025 with these words, spoken by Pope Francis in the his bull of indiction. The pope continues to dwell on the theme "pilgrims of hope," as well as our task to make sense of the present so that it might inspire a real drive toward the future, as we embrace the challenges that arise along the way and dare to give a response. It is precisely the situation in which the world presently finds itself that has inspired the pope's motivation in this exhortation to us all.

As Monsignor Rino Fisichella emphasized during the first Jubilee press conference in June 2022, "Every Holy Year in the history of the Church takes on its full significance when it is placed in the historical [contemporary] context in which humanity lives, especially when it manages to read the signs of the anxieties and fears, together with the expectations, that people perceive. And the fragility experienced in recent years, along with fear of the violence of war, only renders the human condition more paradoxical. On one hand, we have a strong sense of the potential of technology, which dominates our daily lives; Yet on the other hand, we often find ourselves uncertain and confused about the future. From this springs the urgency to live the next Jubilee in the light of hope."

The Jubilee bull is thus titled *Spes non confundit*, recalling the words written two thousand years ago by the Apostle Paul to encourage the Christian community in Rome: "Hope does not disappoint" (Romans 5:5). The foundation of this hope was explained by Pope Francis on May 9, 2024, during the homily given for the celebration in which the document was made public: "Christ, in ascending to heaven, brings to the very heart of God our humanity, with all its hopes and expectations, so that 'we, his members, might be confident of following where he, our Head and Founder, has gone before' [*Preface I of the Acsension of the Lord*]. Brothers and Sisters, it is this hope, based on Christ who died and rose again, that we wish to celebrate, ponder, and proclaim to the whole world in the coming Jubilee. This hope has nothing to do with mere 'human' optimism or the ephemeral expectation of some earthly benefit. No, it is something real, already accomplished in Christ, a gift daily bestowed upon us until the time when we will be one in the embrace of his love."

The pope firmly reiterated that Christian hope "sustains the journey of our lives, even when the road ahead seems winding and exhausting. It opens our eyes to future possibilities whenever resignation or pessimism attempt to imprison us. It makes us see the promise of good at times when evil seems to prevail. Christian hope fills us with serenity when our hearts are burdened by sin and failure. It makes us dream of a new humanity and gives us courage in our efforts to build a fraternal and peaceful world, even when it seems barely worth the effort."

Here his invitation emerges, "[L]et us lift up our hearts to Christ, and become *singers of hope* in a culture marked by much despair. By our actions, our words, the decisions we make each day, our patient efforts to sow seeds of beauty and kindness wherever we find ourselves, we want to sing of hope, so that its melody can touch the heartstrings of humanity and reawaken in every heart the joy and the courage to embrace life to the full. What we—all of us—need, then, is hope."

With detailed elaboration, Pope Francis first addresses what is external: "[H]ope is needed by the society in which we live, often caught up only in the present and incapable of looking to the future. Hope is needed by our age, caught up in an individualism that is frequently content merely to scrape along from day to day. Hope is needed by God's creation, gravely damaged and disfigured by human selfishness. Hope is needed by those peoples and nations who look to the future with anxiety and fear. As injustice and arrogance persist, the poor are discarded, wars sow seeds of death, the least of our brothers and sisters remain at the bottom of the pile, and the dream of a fraternal world seems an illusion."

Yet he does not overlook the interior component: "[H]ope is needed by the Church, so that when she feels wearied by her exertions and burdened by her frailty, she will always remember that, as the Bride of Christ, she is loved with an eternal and faithful love, called to hold high the light of the Gospel, and sent forth to bring to all the fire that Jesus definitively brought to the world." Nor does he allow us to forget: "Each of us has need of hope in our lives, at times so weary and wounded, our hearts thirst for truth, goodness, and beauty, and our dreams that no darkness can dispel. Everything, within and outside of us, cries out for hope and continues to seek, even without knowing it, the closeness of God." Hence his concluding wish: "[M]ay the Lord, risen from the dead and ascended into heaven, grant us the grace to *rediscover* hope, to *proclaim* hope, and to *build* hope."

The Signs of Hope

What Pope Francis offers in the Jubilee bull is not just an empty checklist, but a thoughtful meditation on the signs of the times, emphasizing that these signs, "which include the yearning of human hearts in need of God's saving presence, ought to become signs of hope."

Naturally, the first sign he highlights is peace: "Heedless of the horrors of the past, humanity is confronting yet another ordeal, as many peoples are prey to brutality and violence. How is it possible that their desperate plea for help is not motivating world leaders to resolve the numerous regional conflicts in view of their possible consequences at the global level? Is it too much to dream that arms can fall silent and cease to rain down destruction and death? May the Jubilee remind us that those who are peacemakers will be called 'children of God' (Mt 5:9). The need for peace challenges us all, and demands that concrete steps be taken."

In these challenging circumstances, "Looking to the future with hope also entails having enthusiasm for life and a readiness to share it. Sadly, in many situations this is lacking. A first effect of this is the *loss of desire to transmit life*. [...] Openness to life and responsible parenthood is the design that the Creator has implanted in the hearts and bodies of men and women, a mission that the Lord has entrusted to spouses and to their love." Therefore, the Christian community "should be at the forefront in pointing out the need for a *social covenant to support and foster hope,* one that is inclusive and not ideological, working for a future filled with laughter of babies and children, in order to fill the empty cradles in so many parts of the world."

The pope's precise exhortation, which represents a real challenge for everyone, is to be "tangible signs of hope for those of our brothers and sisters who experience hardships of any kind." His attention turns to the sick, whether at home or in hospitals: "Their sufferings can be allayed by the closeness and affection of those who visit them. Works of mercy are also works of hope that give rise to immense gratitude. Gratitude should likewise be shown to all those healthcare workers who, often in precarious conditions, carry out their mission with constant care and concern for the sick and for those who are most vulnerable." The pope calls to our minds prisoners, "who, deprived of their freedom, daily feel the harshness of detention and its restrictions, lack of affection and, in more than a few cases, lack of respect for their persons. I propose that this Jubilee Year governments undertake initiatives aimed at restoring hope; forms of amnesty or pardon meant to help individuals regain confidence in themselves and in society; and programs of reintegration in the community, including a concrete commitment to respect the law." The pope remembers migrants, "who leave their homelands behind in search of a better life for themselves and for their families. Their expectations must not be frustrated by prejudice and rejection. A spirit of welcome, which embraces everyone with respect for his or her dignity, should be accompanied by a sense of responsibility, lest anyone be denied the right to a dignifies existence. Exiles, displaced persons, and refugees, whom international tensions force to emigrate in order to avoid war, violence and discrimination, ought to be guaranteed security and access to employment and education, the means they need to find their place in a new social context."

Attention is given to the young. "Sadly, they often see their dreams and aspirations frustrated. We must not disappoint them, for the future depends on their enthusiasm. It is gratifying to see the energy they demonstrate, for example, by rolling up their sleeves and volunteering to help when disasters strike and people are in need. Yet it is sad to see young people who are without hope, who face an uncertain and unpromising future, who lack employment or job security, or realistic prospects after finishing school. Without the hope that their dreams can come true, they will inevitably grow discouraged and listless." And likewise, the pope acknowledges the elderly, "who frequently feel lonely and abandoned, [they] also deserve signs of hope. Esteem for the treasure that they are, their life experiences, their accumulated wisdom, and the contribution that they can still make, is incumbent on the Christian community and civil society, which are called to cooperate in strengthening the covenant between generations. Here I would also mention grandparents, who represent the passing on of faith and wisdom to the younger generation. May they find support in the gratitude of their children and the love of their grandchildren, who discover in them their roots and a source of understanding and encouragement."

More broadly, Pope Francis has beckoned "that hope be granted to the billions of the poor, who often lack the essentials of life. Before the constant tide of new forms of impoverishment, we can easily grow inured and resigned. Yet we must not close our eyes to the dramatic situations that we now encounter all around us, not only in certain parts of the world." Here he makes his appeal that "with the money spent on weapons and other military expenditures, let us establish a global fund that can finally put an end to hunger and favor development in the most impoverished countries, so that their citizens will not resort to violent or illusory situations, or have to leave their countries in order to seek a more dignified life." He adds, "I ask that [the more affluent nations] acknowledge the gravity of so many of their past decisions and determine to forgive the debts of countries that will never be able to repay them. More than a question of generosity, this is a matter of justice. It is made all the more serious today by a new form of injustice that we increasingly recognize, namely, that 'a true ecological debt exists, particularly between the global North and South, connected to commercial imbalances with effects on the environment and the disproportionate use of natural resources by certain countries over long periods of time."

In the Spirit of Ecumenism

In 2025, Catholics and Orthodox Christians will celebrate Easter on the same day (April 20), an event that occurs approximately every three years (the previous instance was in 2017, and the next will be in 2028). This is because Western Christians, after the calendar reform enacted by Pope Gregory XIII at the end of 1582, began using the new dating, which aimed to correct the accumulating delay relative to the astronomical first full moon of spring. Eastern Christians, however, continued to determine the date of Easter according to the Julian calendar, introduced by Julius Caesar in 46 BC.

Pope Francis highlights this issue in the Jubilee bull, recalling how the date of Easter was established during the Council of Nicaea in 325. From this, he draws inspiration for his "appeal to all Christians, East and West, to take a decisive step toward unity around a common date for Easter. We do well to remind ourselves that many people, unaware of the controversies of the past, fail to understand how divisions in this regard can continue to exist."

Broadening his view, the pope emphasizes that the Jubilee will also mark the significant commemoration of the 1700th anniversary of that very first great Ecumenical Council, during which about three hundred bishops gathered in the imperial palace of Nicaea (present-day Iznik in Turkey) at the invitation of Emperor Constantine, to compose a creed that would safeguard unity (which was seriously threatened by the denial of the divinity of Jesus Christ and His equality with the Father). This is the Creed still recited at Sunday Mass today.

In Pope Francis' vision, this anniversary should be celebrated as an invitation to individual Christians, "to join in a hymn of praise and thanksgiving to the Blessed Trinity and in particular to Jesus Christ, the Son of God, 'consubstantial with the Father,' who revealed to us that mystery of love." But also the all Churches and Ecclesial Communities "to persevere on the path to visible unity and in the quest of finding ways to respond fully to the prayer of Jesus 'that they may all be one. As you, Father, are in me and I am in you, may they also be in us, so that the world may believe that you have sent me' (Jn 17:21)."

Building on this, Francis reflects on the heart of the Christian faith—Jesus' death and resurrection—and the cornerstone of Christian hope—namely, eternal life. This is clearly annunciated by the Second Vatican Council: "Without a religious foundation and the hope of eternal life, human dignity is gravely imperiled, as we often see today, and the mysteries of life and death, guilt and suffering remain unsolved, leading many people to despair." The pope expands on this: "[B]y virtue of the hope in which we are saved, can view the passage of time with the certainty that the history of humanity and our own individual history are not doomed to a dead end or a dark abyss, but directed to an encounter with the Lord of glory. As a result, we live our lives in expectation of his return and in the hope of living forever in him."

Christian hope, the pope firmly asserts, consists precisely in this: "[T]hat in facing death, which appears to be the end of everything, we have the certainty that, thanks to the grace of God imparted to us in Baptism, 'life is changed, not ended,' forever. Buried with Christ in Baptism, we receive in his resurrection the gift of a new life that breaks down the walls of death, making it a passage to eternity. The reality of death, as a painful separation from those dearest to us, cannot be mitigated by empty rhetoric. The Jubilee, however, offers us the opportunity to appreciate anew, and with immense gratitude, the gift of the new life that we have received in Baptism, a life capable of transfiguring death's drama."

In the ecumenical dimension, "The most convincing testimony to this hope is provided by the martyrs. Steadfast in their faith in the risen Christ, they rennounced life itself here below, rather than betray their Lord. Martyrs, as confessors of the life that knows no end, are present and numerous in every age, and perhaps even more so in our own day. We need to treasure their testimony, in order to confirm our hope and allow it to bear good fruit. The martyrs, coming as they do from different Christian traditions, are also seeds of unity, expressions of the ecumenism of blood. I greatly hope that the Jubilee will also include ecumenical celebrations as a way of highlighting the richness of the testimony of these martyrs."

Beyond simply looking back at previous Holy Years, Pope Francis is already oriented toward the future, directing our path toward another significant milestone for all Christians: "2033 will mark the two thousandth anniversary of the redemption won by the passion, death, and resurrection of the Lord Jesus. We are about to make a pilgrimage marked by great events, in which the grace of God precedes and accompanies his people as they press forward firm in faith, active in charity, and steadfast in hope."

The Signs of the Jubilee

Archbishop Rino Fisichella, pro-prefect of the Dicastery for Evangelization, to whom Pope Francis entrusted the organization of the Jubilee 2025, writes: "A pilgrimage is not a prerogative of Christianity. One might say it belongs to the history of humanity. Where there is man, there is his 'embarking on the way.'"

However, within Christianity, the pilgrimage has given special significance to the notion of 'sign,' expressed in three dimensions—namely, the call, the promise, and the certainty of fulfillment (which also characterized the ritual pilgrimages of the Israelites): "A pilgrimage as an act of faith undoubtedly begins with a personal call in which we are asked to set out on a journey to follow what God has determined for each of us. In this way, the believer is open and ready to discover the content of the promise made him and will be able to grow and move into the fullness of his existence in the hope of his fulfillment."

A document published several years ago by the Pontifical Council for the Pastoral Care of Migrants clarifies the meaning of pilgrimage: "A pilgrimage symbolizes the experience of the *homo viator* ["man on his way"] who, as soon as he leaves his mother's womb, embarks on the journey through time and space of his existence; the fundamental experience of Israel, marching toward the promised land of salvation and total freedom; the experience of Christ, who ascends from the land of Jerusalem to Heaven, opening the way to the Father; the experience of the Church, moving through history toward the heavenly Jerusalem; and the experience of all humanity, striving toward hope and fulfillment."

The official Jubilee website explains: "The Jubilee calls for us to embark on a journey and cross certain boundaries. When we move, we don't just change our location, we transform ourselves. This is why it is important to prepare, plan the route, and know the destination. In this sense, the pilgrimage of this year begins before the journey itself: its starting point is the decision to actually make it. The etymology of the word 'pilgrimage' is quite rich and has undergone few changes in meaning. The word derives from the Latin *per ager*, meaning 'through the fields,' or *per eger*, meaning 'border crossing': both roots remind us of the defining aspect of embarking on a journey."

The pilgrimage to the four major basilicas (St. Peter's in the Vatican, St. John Lateran, St. Mary Major, and St. Paul Outside the Walls) is an explicit sign of the Jubilee experience, as it symbolizes the journey that every person makes in this mortal life, as is passing through the threshold the Holy Doors. Pope Francis emphasizes this as well: "Life is a pilgrimage, and the human being is a *viator*, a pilgrim walking toward the desired goal. It will be a sign that mercy is also a goal to reach, something requiring commitment and sacrifice. The pilgrimage, therefore, might be seen as a stimulus for conversion: crossing the threshold of the Holy Door, we allow ourselves to be embraced by God's mercy and commit ourselves to being merciful to others as the Father is merciful to us."

For this reason, the first rite that characterizes every Jubilee is the opening of the Holy Doors, which provides a special point of access to the four papal basilicas that is accessible only during Holy Years. This explicitly symbolizes what the Church offers during this particular time of grace—that is, an "extraordinary" path in the journey of conversion toward salvation. Specifically, it references the passage from sin to grace, in the light of Christ who, in the parable of the Good Shepherd, says of Himself: "I am the door; whoever enters through me will be saved" (John 10:9).

Six centuries ago, during the Jubilee of 1425, Pope Martin V inaugurated this tradition by opening the Holy Door at St. John Lateran. Until 1975, the Holy Doors were sealed both externally and internally in the basilicas. In that year, Pope Paul VI was the last to strike the wall three times with a hammer and tear the wall down. Later, wanting to shift attention from the wall to the Holy Door itself, he decided that it should no longer be sealed from the outside behind a wall. Therefore, at the end of that Jubilee, the traditional silver trowel used to start the sealing process was no longer employed and no wall of closure erected in front of the door.

Similarly, the demolition of the internal wall is no longer symbolically initiated by the pope and then continued by masons. Beginning in 1950, the wall is dismantled beforehand, and during the solemn liturgical hymns the pope pushes the door open from the outside. He himself is then the first pilgrim to pass through it, emphasizing that the Jubilee pilgrimage is not a private, individual act, but a sign of the journey of the whole people of God toward the Kingdom.

These are the words used by the pope (or his delegate) during the opening rite as he strikes the Holy Door, and they express the spiritual meaning of the gesture: *Aperite mihi portam iustitiae* ("Open for me the gates of justice"). This is an explicit reference to the ancient biblical hymn of thanksgiving and praise: "Open for me the gates of righteousness; I will enter and give thanks to the Lord. This is the gate of the Lord through which the righteous may enter" (Psalm 118:19–20).

As Pope Francis clarifies in the bull of indiction of the Extraordinary Year of Mercy in 2015: "Mercy is not opposed to justice but rather expresses God's way of reaching out to the sinner, offering him a new chance to look at himself, convert, and believe […]. God's justice is his mercy given to everyone as grace that flows from the death and resurrection of Jesus Christ. Thus the Cross of Christ is God's judgment on all of us and on the whole world, because through it he offers us the certitude of love and new life" (*Misericordiae vultus*, n. 21).

Furthermore, as the official website notes, "In passing through this threshold, the pilgrim is reminded of the text of chapter 10 of John's gospel: 'I am the door; whoever enters through me will be saved; he will come in and go out and find pasture.' The gesture expresses the decision to follow and be guided by Jesus who is the Good Shepherd. Moreover, the door is also the passage that introduces one into the church. For the Christian community, it is not only a sacred space to be approached with respect, appropriate behavior, and dress, but it is a sign of the communion that binds each believer to Christ: it is the place of encounter and dialogue, reconciliation, and peace awaiting the visit of each and every pilgrim—the space of the Church as the community of the faithful."

The Jubilee Year Logo

The logo of the Holy Year 2025 was designed by graphic artist Giacomo Travisani, winner of an international competition wherein 294 people across 48 countries participated. As Archbishop Fisichella explains, the criteria by which the committee selected three project finalists were threefold: Entries were to be "pastoral, such that the message of the Jubilee be easily intuited; technical in that the graphics could be easily reproduced and rendered; and aesthetical, that the design is well done and catches the eye." The ultimate choice was then personally made by Pope Francis himself in a private audience on 11 June 2022.

The organizing committee proposed a theological interpretation that is quite detailed: "The logo represents four figures stylized in a manner that indicates humanity coming from four corners of the earth. They embrace each other indicating solidarity and fraternity that must join all people together. One notes that the figure first in line clutches the cross—this is the sign not only of the faith that embraces, but of the hope that can never be abandoned because we have constant need of it, above all in those moments of greatest necessity. It is helpful to observe the waves underneath and are placed there as marks of the pilgrimage of life that is not always smooth sailing. Often personal affairs and world events bear upon us and urge us to lean on our hope intensely. For this reason one must underline the lower ends of the cross that extend outward and form a kind of anchor to be cast into the troubled water. As one knows, this is not the first time the anchor has been used as a sign of hope. The anchor of hope, in fact, is the name that in nautical jargon is used for the back-up anchor used by the water vessels to undertake emergency maneuvers and to stabilize the vessel during a storm. One cannot overlook the fact that the image shows just how much the way of the pilgrim is not a solitary path but one taken in common, marked by its growing dynamism that ever bends toward the cross. The cross is not at all static, but is itself likewise dynamic: it curves toward humanity as if to initiate an encounter and not leave them alone, offering the certainty of presence and security of hope."

The author later explained having envisioned "people of every color, nationality, and culture pressing in from four corners of the earth and moving toward the future, fellow human beings, and the world, like the sail of a great ship we are all on, moved by the grace of the wind of hope that is the Cross of Christ, Christ Himself. And the pope [as he imagined], Peter for today, guides the people of God toward the common center, embracing the cross that will become an anchor—the lodestar for all of humanity—and we the people strive among ourselves toward him as if we too were strapped to that anchor, symbolically evoking pilgrims of every time and place." With respect to the color scheme, Travisani specified that "red is for love, in both action and as it is shared; yellow-orange stands for human warmth; green evokes peace and balance; the blue indicates security and protection; lastly, the gray-black of the cross and anchor represents the eminent and interior aspect, a light in which one might even lose himself."

The Jubilee Hymn

The hymn of the Holy Year 2025, titled "Pilgrims of Hope" after the motto of this Jubilee, was written by Monsignor Pierangelo Sequeri and composed by Maestro Francesco Meneghello, the winner of an international competition in which 270 individuals from 38 different nations participated. (The hymn can be downloaded in various language versions at the following link: www.iubilaeum2025.va/it/giubileo-2025/inno-giubileo-2025.html.)

According to the description provided on the official website, the hymn's text draws inspiration primarily from passages of the prophet Isaiah, with themes of creation, fraternity, God's tenderness, and hope: "Step by step, the people of faith in their daily pilgrimage confidently lean on the source of Life. The song that arises spontaneously during the journey is directed to God. It is a song filled with the hope of being freed and sustained. It is a song accompanied by the wish that it may reach the ears of the One who makes it flow. It is God who, like an ever-living flame, keeps hope alive and gives strength to the steps of the people who walk."

The authors further explain: "Christian hope is dynamic and illuminates the pilgrimage of life, revealing the faces of brothers and sisters, fellow travelers on the journey. It is not a wandering of lone wolves, but a journey of people, confident and joyful, moving toward a new destination. The breath of the Spirit of life never fails to light up the dawn of the future that is on the rise. The heavenly Father watches with patience and tenderness the pilgrimage of His children and opens the Way for them, pointing to Jesus, His Son, who becomes the path for all."

Chorus
Like a flame my hope is burning,
      may my song arise to you:
Source of life that has no ending,
      on life's path I trust in you.

Verse 1
Ev'ry nation, tongue, and people
      find a light within your Word.
Scattered fragile sons and daughters
      find a home in your dear Son.

Verse 2
God, so tender and so patient,
      dawn of hope, you care for all.
Heav'n and earth are recreated
      by the Spirit of Life set free.

Verse 3
Raise your eyes, the wind is blowing,
      for our God is born in time.
Son made man for you and many
      who will find the way in him.

The Jubilee Churches in Rome

In the bull of indiction, Pope Francis explains that the Jubilee churches "serve as oases of spirituality and places of rest on the pilgrimage of faith, where one can drink from the wellsprings of hope, above all by approaching the sacrament of Reconciliation, the essential starting-point of any true journey of conversion." To this end, visits to numerous places of worship throughout Rome are encouraged, places chosen both for their specific spiritual significance and for their connections to the different nationalities of pilgrims.

For those unable to make the journey to Rome, three basilicas in the Holy Land are also noted (the Holy Sepulcher in Jerusalem, the Church of the Nativity in Bethlehem, and the Church of the Annunciation in Nazareth); the two basilicas in Assisi (San Francesco and Santa Maria degli Angeli); those dedicated to Our Lady (the Holy House in Loreto, the Shrine of the Blessed Virgin of the Rosary in Pompeii); the Basilica of St. Anthony in Padua; all minor basilicas, cathedrals, or co-cathedrals; Marian shrines or other significant churches designated by a diocesan bishop, as well as national or international shrines specified by an episcopal conference.

Here is a brief description of the Jubilee churches in Rome (in addition to the seven churches mentioned in chapter three that comprise the traditional "pilgrimage of the seven churches").

Santo Spirito in Sassia (via dei Penitenzieri 12): This is located where the Saxons built a chapel and hospice for their pilgrims in the 8th century. It has been the center of the spirituality of the Divine Mercy since 1994, a devotion linked to the apparitions and interior inspirations of St. Faustina Kowalska.

Sant'Andrea delle Fratte (via di Sant'Andrea delle Fratte 1): Built in the 17th century, this church features a chapel that commemorates the 1842 apparition of the Madonna of the Miraculous Medal to Alphonse Ratisbonne, who converted to Catholicism and later became a priest.

Sanctuary of Madonna del Divino Amore (via del Santuario 10): A pilgrimage site since 1740, it is associated with a miraculous intervention of Our Lady who saved a lost pilgrim from wild dogs. A new sanctuary was consecrated by Pope John Paul II in 1999.

San Paolo alla Regola (piazza di San Paolo alla Regola 6): Dating back to the 4th century, this church is traditionally said to be located where the Apostle Paul once stayed. It has been used by the Bulgarian Orthodox community since 2014, who with the permission of the vicariate of Rome celebrate divine liturgy here on Sunday.

San Salvatore in Lauro (piazza di San Salvatore in Lauro): This church was founded around the year 1000 and for centuries guided by the "Celestine" monks (canons regular of St. George in Alga). In 1668 responsibility for the church passed to a foundation, Pio Sodalizio dei Piceni; today the church is known for its devotion to Our Lady of Loreto.

Santa Maria in Vallicella (via del Governo Vecchio 134): Built at the end of the sixth century, this is home to the miraculous fresco of the Madonna, which bled after being struck by a stone in the 14th century. Since 1575, it has been under the care of the Oratorians, founded by St. Philip Neri.

Santa Maria dell'Orazione e Morte (via Giulia 262): Built in the sixteenth century by a confraternity of the same name that buried abandoned bodies, its cemetery was operational until the 19th century. It contains over eight thousand corpses drawn from the Tiber or surrounding fields.

Santa Caterina da Siena (via Giulia 151): Originally built in 1526 for the Sienese Confraternity, the church was later rebuilt in the second half of the 1800s under Sienese architect Paolo Posi.

Spirito Santo dei Napoletani (via Giulia 34): Taken over by the Neapolitan Confraternity in 1572, this church was restored by architect Domenico Fontana. In the 1800s it was the national church of the Kingdom of the Two Sicilies.

Santa Maria del Suffragio (via Giulia 59 A): Built as the headquarters of the confraternity of the same name, it is dedicated to praying for the souls of the deceased. The church was refurbished in 1594 by Pope Clement VIII.

San Giovanni Battista dei Fiorentini (via Acciaioli 2): Constructed in the 16th century, it boasts contributions from notable architects like Bramante, Raphael, and Borromini. The latter two are buried here. Its first rector was St. Philip Neri at the request of the Florentines who desired it for their national church.

Santa Maria in Monserrato (via di Monserrato 115): Built in 1506 for Spanish pilgrims under the direction of the confraternity of the Virgin of Monserrat in Catalogna and architect Antonio da Sangallo the younger, this church contains works by Bernini and Carracci.

Santi Silvestro e Martino ai Monti (viale del Monte Oppio 28): Founded in the 4th century by Pope Silvester I, it was originally an oratory dedicated to all martyrs, but was rebuilt at the end of the fifth century by Pope Symmachus who dedicated it to St. Silvester and St. Martin of Tours. Later relics of martyrs from the Catacombs of Priscilla were deposited here.

Santa Prisca (via di Santa Prisca 11): Dedicated to the daughter of Aquila and Priscilla, mentioned in the Acts of the Apostles. It houses her relics, discovered in the 3rd century. She was baptized by St. Paul at the age of thirteen and martyred during the reign of Emperor Claudio by decapitation after being left alone and untouched by wild beasts in Circus Maximus and surviving tortures at the stake.

Santa Maria della Vittoria (via XX Settembre 17): This church was designed by Carlo Moderno and given its present name after originally being dedicated to St. Paul. The church was dedicated to Our Lady after a Catholic victory at Montagna Bianca in 1620 in Prague during in the Thirty Years' War. (Ferdinand II fought the Protestants under Frederick V of the Palatinate.) It is famous for the *Ecstasy of Saint Teresa* by Gian Lorenzo Bernini.

Trinità dei Monti (piazza della Trinità dei Monti 3): Built by

King Charles VIII of France as a gesture of gratitude toward Francesco di Paola to house the friars minor founded by the latter. The church's seventeen chapels were sponsored by noble Roman families and have been supported by these since their origins.

Santa Cecilia in Trastevere (piazza di Santa Cecilia 22): According to tradition, this church is built on the site of St. Cecilia's home, virgin martyr around the year 230. In the 16th century, during an excavation of the house and the body it contained, the discovery of an inexplicably persevered and intact corpse was discovered, and in the posture reproduced in the stature sculpted by Stefano Maderno, which can be seen today under the main altar.

Sant'Agostino in Campo Marzio (piazza di Sant'Agostino): Built in the fifteenth century by Augustinian monks in honor of the saint who inspired their Rule. It is known for housing the *Madonna of Loreto* by Caravaggio, Raffael's *The Prophet Isaiah,* Jacopo Sansovino's statue *Madonna del Parto,* and other important works of art.

Special attention is also being given to 'national churches,' places of worship that have been historically tied to specific countries for cultural or artistic reasons, or those that have traditionally welcomed pilgrims from individual countries or regions. These include:

Albania—San Giovanni della Malva in Trastevere (*Piazza di San Giovanni della Malva*). Here the litugy is celebrated in the Albanian language according to the Latin rite.

Argentina—Santa Maria Addolorata at Piazza Buenos Aires (*Viale Regina Margherita 81*). This church was founded in 1910 by the Argentinian priest José León Gallardo with the donations from the bishops of his country.

Armenia—San Nicola da Tolentino (*Via di San Nicola da Tolentino 17*). Here one finds the tomb of the first cardinal of Armenia, Gregorio Pietro Agagianian.

Austria and Germany—Santa Maria dell'Anima (*Via di Santa Maria dell'Anima 64*). This historiclly has been closely linked to the Hapsburg family.

Belgium—San Giuliano dei Fiamminghi (*Via del Sudario 40*). This chapel was founded in the eleventh century by the Flemmish community in Rome.

Canada—Nostra Signora del Santissimo Sacramento e dei Santi Martiri Canadesi [Our Lady of the Most Holy Sacrament and of the Canadian Martyrs] (*Via Giovanni Battista de Rossi 46*). This church was consecrated in 1962 by Cardinal Paul-Émmile Léger, archbishop of Montreal.

China—San Bernardino in Panisperna (*Via Panisperna 256*). In 2003 Mass was celebrated here in the Chinese language and houses a meeting center named after Augustine Chao, Chinese martyr of the eighteenth century.

Cyprus—Santa Maria in via Lata (*Via del Corso 306*). This is situated on the spot where it is claimed that St. Paul's prison was located, where he landed after his sojourn in the Mediterranean.

Croatia—San Girolamo dei Croati (*Via Tomacelli 132*). Built under orders of Pope Sixtus V, originally from Croatia, it is named after the protector-saint of Illyria.

Denmark—Santa Maria in Transpotina (*Via della Conciliazione 14 C*). Originally, this was a chapel erected in the seventeenth century in honor of the nation's saint, King Knut.

Eritrea—San Tommaso in Parione (*Via di Parione 29*). Here the liturgy is celebrated in the Alexandrian rite.

Estonia—Santa Sabina all'Aventino (*Piazza Pietro d'Illiria 1*). This has been under the care of the Domenicans since the thirteenth century. The Domenicans are very active in the capital city, Tallinn.

Phillipines—Santa Prudenziana (*Via Urbana 160*). This is the headquarters of the chaplaincy and mission for Philippino migrants.

Finland—Santa Maria sopra Minerva (*Piazza della Minerva 42*). On 19 January every year the memorial of Saint Eric of Uppsala is celebrated, bishop and patron of Finland.

France—San Luigi dei Francesi (*Piazza de San Luigi dei Francesi*). This church was founded in 1518 by Giulio Cardinal Medici, later Pope Clement VII, for the service of the French community in Rome.

Japan—Santa Maria dell'Orto [Our Lady of the Garden] (*Via Anicia 10*). This is the Marian title traditionally attributed to the protection recieved by Japanese dignitaries during a storm at sea near Ostia in the sixteenth century.

Great Britain—San Tommaso di Canterbury (*Via di Monserrato*). This has been the place of refuge for English pilgrims since the twelfth century.

Hungary—Santo Stefano Rotondo (*Via Santo Stefano Rotondo 7*). This church was entrusted to the Hungarian Paulist Order in the fifteenth century. The main altar is dedicated to the saints of the royal family of the Árpád.

India—Sant'Anastasia al Palatino (*Piazza di Sant'Anastasia 1*). Here the Indian community celebrates the liturgy in the Syro-Malabar rite.

Ireland—Sant'Isidoro a Capo le Case (*Via degli Artisti 41*). This church was acquired in 1624 by Irish Franciscans who fled their home country during a period of Protestant persecution.

Italy—Santa Maria degli Angeli e dei Martiri [Our Lady of the Angels and Martyrs] (*Piazza della Repubblica*). This basilica is used for many official clebrations of the Italian Republic.

Latvia—Santi Quattro Coronati (*Via dei Santi Quattro 20*). This church's titular cardinal patron was between 1983 and 1990 the Latvian Archbishop Julijans Vaivods.

Lebanon—San Marone (*Via Aurora 6*). This church is dedicated to the hermit and founder of the Maronite Church of the fifth century; the rite of Antioch is used and celebrated in the Arab language.

Lithuania—Chiesa del Gesù (*Piazza del Gesù*). This church contains the tomb of Bishop Vilnius Jerzy Radziwill (1556–1600), the first Lithuanian cardinal.

Luxemburg—Sacro Cuore di Gesù (*Via Marsala 42*). This country has a strong devotion to the Sacred Heart due in large part to the efforts of the Barnabite Antonio Maresca.

Malta—San Paolo alle Tre Fontane (*Via di Acque Salvie 1*). Here the three months St. Paul spent preaching on the island around the year 60 is commemorated.

Mexico—Nostro Signora di Guadalupe e San Filippo (*Via Aurelia 675*). This is dedicated to the Virgin Patroness of the country and to St. Felipe de las Casas, the first Mexican saint who was martyred in Japan in 1597.

Netherlands—Santi Michele e Magno (*Largo degli Alicorni 21*). Standing since the ninth century, this chapel was established by the Frisians who converted to Christianity.

Poland—San Stanislao (*Via delle Botteghe Oscure 15*). This church was built in 1578 by the Polish Stanislaus Cardinal Osio in honor of the patron of Poland, Stanislaw Szczepanowski.

Portugal—Sant'Antonio dei Portoghesi (*Via dei Portoghesi 2*). Antonio Cardinal Martinez de Chaves established this church in 1445 where Portuguese pilgrims were already welcomed and housed.

Czech Republic—San Clemente (*Piazza di San Clemente*). This church is the home of the relics of St. Cyril, who together with his brother, St. Methodius, is particularly important to the Czech community.

Romania—San Salvatore alle Coppelle (*Via delle Coppelle 72 B*). This has been the national church of the Romanian Greek Catholics since 1914, and the liturgy is celebrated in the Byzantine rite.

Russia—Sant'Antonio Abate all'Esquilino (*Via Carlo Alberto 2*). This is the location of the Pontifical College, the *Russicum,* and place of meeting for Russian Catholics of the Byzantine rite.

Slovakia—Santa Prassede (*Via di Santa Prassede 9 A*). This is the site of the monestary where Sts. Cyril and Methodius lived, patrons of Slavic people and translators of the Bible into the Slavic characters.

Slovenia—Santa Maria Maggiore (*Piazza di Santa Maria Maggiore*). This is where Pope Adrian II welcomed Sts. Cyril and Methodius in 867 and approved the liturgical books written in the Slavic languages.

Spain—San Pietro in Montorio (*Piazza di San Pietro in Montorio 3*). This was financed by Spanish royals, Ferdinand V and Isabelle of Castile, at the end of the fifteenth century, to mark the fulfillment of their petition for the birth of an heir.

Sweden—Santa Brigida (*Piazza Farnese 96*). This is built onto the structure wherein St. Bridget of Sweden lived with her daughter, Catherine, in the second half of the fourteenth century.

Ukraine—Santi Sergio e Bacco (*Piazza della Madonna dei Monti 3*). This has been the cathedral of the Apostolic Exarchate for Ukrainian Catholics of the Byzantine rite.

United States—San Patrizio a Villa Ludovisi (*Vis Boncompagni 31*). This church is managed by the Priestly Missionaries of Saint Paul Apostle, and in 2017 it was subsumed into the care the church Santa Susanna, whose pastoral care is provided by the United States.

A Year of Events

The official calendar only includes events organized by the Vatican Jubilee Committee for different groups. To attend specific events at St. Peter's Basilica, free tickets must be requested at: https://eventi.pontificalisdomus.va/?lang=en-us. Access to St. Peter's Square will remain open, with large screens allowing attendees to follow along with the ceremonies and the Eucharistic celebrations underway.

2024

December 24: Opening of the Holy Door of St. Peter's Basilica in the Vatican
December 25: Christmas
December 29: Opening of the Holy Door at St. John Lateran and in all cathedrals and co-cathedrals around the world

2025

January 1: Opening of the Holy Door at the Basilica of St. Mary Major
January 5: Opening of the Holy Door at the Basilica of St. Paul Outside the Walls
January 24–26: Jubilee for the world of communications

February 8–9: Jubilee for the armed forces, police, and security personnel
February 16–18: Jubilee for artists
February 21–23: Jubilee for deacons

March 8–9: Jubilee for the world of volunteer work
March 28: 24 Hours for the Lord initiative
March 28–30: Jubilee for the missionaries of mercy

April 5–6: Jubilee for the sick and the world of healthcare
April 20: Easter
April 25–27: Jubilee for adolescents
April 28–30: Jubilee for people with disabilities

May 1–4: Jubilee for workers
May 4–5: Jubilee for entrepreneurs
May 10–11: Jubilee for musical bands

May 16–18: Jubilee for confraternities
May 24–25: Jubilee for children
May 30–31: Jubilee for families, grandparents, and the elderly

June 1: Jubilee for families, grandparents, and the elderly
June 7–8: Jubilee for movements, associations, and new communities
June 9: Jubilee for the Holy See
June 14–15: Jubilee for the world of sports
June 20–22: Jubilee for government officials
June 23–24: Jubilee for seminarians
June 25: Jubilee for bishops
June 25–27: Jubilee for priests
June 28: Jubilee for Eastern Churches

July 28–31: Jubilee for young people

August 1–3: Jubilee for young people

September 15: Jubilee of consolation
September 20: Jubilee for justice workers
September 26–28: Jubilee for catechists

October 5: Jubilee for migrants
October 8–9: Jubilee for consecrated life
October 11–12: Jubilee for Marian spirituality
October 18–19: Jubilee for the missionary world
October 30–3: Jubilee for the world of education

November 1–2: Jubilee for the world of education
November 16: Jubilee for the poor
November 22–23: Jubilee for choirs and choral groups

December 14: Jubilee for prisoners

December 28: Closing of the Holy Doors at St. John Lateran, St. Mary Major, and St. Paul Outside the Walls

2026

January 6: Closing of the Holy Door at St. Peter's Basilica in the Vatican

2

INDULGENCE: FRUIT OF THE JUBILEE EXPERIENCE

What Is an Indulgence?

The indulgence "allows us to discover how limitless God's mercy is. It is no coincidence that in ancient times the term 'mercy' was interchangeable with 'indulgence,' as it expresses the fullness of God's forgiveness, which knows no bounds." In this summary provided by Pope Francis, we grasp the true meaning of a word that, throughout history, has been misunderstood and subject to controversy—so much so that it was one of the catalysts of the Protestant Reformation, initiated by Martin Luther in 1517 in opposition to the excessive sale of spiritual benefits during that time.

To understand its current relevance, one must keep in mind that indulgences are inherent to the relationship between theology and spirituality—that is, between penitential acts and pastoral care. They require personal freedom and responsibility, as indulgences are linked to specific works that must be performed. Pope Paul VI provides the solemn ecclesiastical definition in his apostolic constitution *Indulgentiarum doctrina* (a fundamental definition that is repeated in the *Catechism of the Catholic Church*, no. 1471): "An indulgence is a remission before God of the temporal punishment due to sins whose guilt has already been forgiven, which the faithful Christian who is duly disposed gains under certain conditions through the action of the Church which, as the minister of redemption, dispenses and applies with authority the treasury of the satisfactions of Christ and the saints."

In essence, through the sacrament of confession the sinner receives forgiveness from God for his or her sins, but one must still undertake the correlative temporal punishment for sins committed, either through penance on earth or in purgatory. This theological distinction between guilt and punishment is key to understanding indulgences, which at first glance might seem like a outdated custom with a medieval flair. One must approach this notion with an outlook in faith—a perspective that gazes beyond the earthly horizon and engages the mysteries that follow death, in full awareness of the soul's immortality.

As Mauro Cardinal Piacenza, the emeritus Major Penitentiary, notes, "Indulgences are incomprehensible to the secularized person, and even to some Christians who, in the name of demystifying Christianity, have reduced it to an ethical doctrine useful only for modern states to maintain their power. The indulgence is, instead, a hymn to freedom, a full recognition of human dignity, given that humans—being rational, free, and capable of willing—are responsible for their own actions. The Last Judgment will not be the 'wiping clean' of history. Thus, the persistence of temporal punishment, even after sacramental absolution, makes each person aware of the consequences of his actions and indicates the individual responsibility to make amends. More importantly, it calls everyone to participate in Christ's redemptive work for oneself and for others."

To understand indulgences correctly, we must look beyond earthly definitions of "justice" and "mercy" and consider them in the light of the absolute goodness of God. As Pope Francis explains in the bull issued for the 2015 Jubilee, "These are not two contradictory realities, but two dimensions of a single reality that unfolds progressively until it culminates in the fullness of love. Justice is a fundamental concept for civil society, which is meant to be governed by the rule of law. Justice is also understood as that which is rightly due to each individual. In the Bible, there are many references to divine justice and to God as a 'judge.' In these passages, justice is understood as the full observance of the Law and the behavior of every good Israelite in conformity with God's commandments. Such a vision, however, has not infrequently led to legalism by distorting the original meaning of justice and obscuring its profound value. To overcome this legalistic perspective, we need to recall that in Sacred Scripture, justice is conceived essentially as the faithful abandonment to oneself to God's will."

Requirements for Receiving an Indulgence

To gain a *plenary* indulgence (which according to the doctrine of the Church is different than the *partial* indulgence), as is possible in a Jubilee year, there are three main conditions: the sacrament of reconciliation (confession), the sacrament of the Eucharist (communion), and prayer for the pope's intentions. Partial indulgences can be obtained, for example, by reciting certain indulgence prayers.

In confession, when penitents have hearts detached from any sin, the faithful approach the threshold of the Mystery, draw closer to God and thereby allow Him to come closer to them. In this sacrament, the penitent lets Christ the Good Samaritan lower himself and heal the wounds of the penitent through the redemption realized in the sacrifice on the cross.

Celebrating the Eucharist and sacramental communion emphasizes the ecclesial dimension of the indulgence, a matter of reflection for supernatural communion. This is a gift of the Holy Spirit and is communion with the entire Church.

Prayer for the pope's intentions reminds us that this communion is not merely spiritual but is also a concrete union with "our Holy Mother and hierarchical Church." As Pope Francis often emphasizes, the first duty of the successor of St. Peter is to pray for the Church. Therefore, those seeking the indulgence are called to unite their prayers with those of the pope, rendering their prayers universal.

It is advisable to receive communion and pray for the pope's intentions on the same day as the Jubilee pilgrimage, but these conditions can also be fulfilled before or after the pilgrimage (typically within about twenty days).

During the pious pilgrimage to a Jubilee site, according to the indications of the Apostolic Penitentiary, the faithful should devoutly participate in the Holy Mass or, alternatively, in the Liturgy of the Word, the Liturgy of the Hours (office of readings, lauds, vespers), the Stations of the Cross, the Marian rosary, or the *Akáthistos* hymn, or a penance service that concludes with individual confessions. Lastly, pilgrims are instructed to spend an appropriate amount of time in Eucharistic adoration and meditation, ending with the Lord's Prayer, a Profession of Faith, and invocations to Our Lady, the Mother of God.

Additionally, Jubilee indulgences can be obtained by participating with a committed soul in parish missions, spiritual exercises, or formation meetings elaborating on the texts of the Second Vatican Council or the *Catechism of the Catholic Church* (and these should be conducted in a church or other suitable place). It is also recommended that one perform works of mercy and penance, by which the pilgrim gives witness to his desire for conversion: the indulgence is obtained then when one visits his neighbor in need (the sick, prisoners, or those in need, including the disabled and homebound, etc.). This is as if to make a pilgrimage to Christ present in these people in difficulty, and also fulfill the usual spiritual conditions in the sacraments and prayer.

A further opportunity available during this Jubilee is linked to the initiative that draws in a concrete and generous way from the penitential spirit that characterizes the Jubilee. This means a rediscovery of the penitential value of Fridays: in a spirit of penance avoiding frivolous distractions (actual and virtual, for example social media) or overindulging (fasting or abstinence according to general norms of the Church and specifications given by individual bishops), and also remembering the poor in their needs. On this day one is attentive to works that are religious or social in nature, especially efforts to defend and protect life in all stages as well as the quality of existence—whether it be aimed at abandoned children, youth in hardship, elderly in need or isolated, migrants from various places in search of a better life for themselves and their families. One also might dedicate an appropriate amount of free time to volunteer service that focuses on the interests of the community, or other works of self-initiative.

For those who cannot physically participate in pilgrimages or attend celebrations due to illness, age, or other limitations (cloistered religious, for example, or the infirm and recluse), the indulgence can still be received if they unite themselves spiritually to the celebrations and Church prayers, especially during times when the pope or local bishops' words are broadcast through the media. The faithful may wherever they find themselves recite the Our Father, Profession of Faith in a legitimate form, and other prayers conforming to the objectives of this Holy Year and offer up the inconveniences and suffering of their lives.

Pope Francis expressed the hope during the 2015 Jubilee that "the Jubilee indulgence may reach everyone as a genuine experience of God's mercy, which extends toward us all with the face of a Father who welcomes and forgives, completely forgetting the sin committed." He also reiterated that indulgences can be obtained for the deceased. "We are bound to them through the witness of faith and charity that they have left us. As we remember them in the Eucharistic celebration, so may we in the great mystery of the communion of saints pray for them so that the merciful gaze of the Father frees them from all trace of sin and might draw them to Himself in the beatitude that has no end."

The Three Aspects of Sin

In Saint Augustine's concise definition, sin is "a word, act, or desire contrary to the eternal law." As explained in the *Compendium of the Catechism of the Catholic Church*, sin "is an offense against God, a disobedience to His love; it wounds human nature and harms human solidarity." In essence, sin is the denial of the good, a renunciation, or even a deliberate rejection of the good, in the guise of fruitless self-interest. There can be no moral or doctrinal compromise with sin or the enslavement it always brings.

There are three key passages in the Bible that illustrate the different aspects of sin. Above all is Genesis 3:1–24. This well-known episode features Adam and Eve being tempted by the diabolical serpent, who convinces them to succumb to their desires and eat the forbidden fruit, leading to their expulsion from the Garden of Eden. This story highlights the aspect of falling to temptation, which Satan introduces through lies, portraying evil as good and as a means of self-elevation. This deception shifts the focus from the objective to the subjective, where what only seems right to the individual (the "I") replaces what is objectively good, true, and just (God). It is easy to see how this fundamental distortion leads to other corruptions, including violations of the natural order. Thus, sin is diametrically opposed to worship—that is, the practical recognition of God as the one and only Absolute.

A further passage in Exodus 32:1–14 recounts the incident of the golden calf, which was fashioned by Aaron and worshiped by the Israelites while Moses was receiving the Ten Commandments on Mount Sinai. Here, sin is represented by the attempt to bring God down to a manageable level, turning Him into something easily within one's grasp as utterly tangible and thereby denying His transcendence. This leads to idolatry—'constructing' a god out of something molded by human hands. In every grave sin, there is an element of idolatry, the worship of something created that becomes the ultimate reference

point—whether it be money, power, sex, or ideologies of any kind—
to which one sacrifices people, principles, and values.

Lastly, Ezekiel 16:1–63 presents a metaphorical account of Israel's sin of adultery through the worship of foreign gods, particularly those from neighboring polytheistic nations. Whereas Genesis
highlights pride and disobedience as the roots of sin, and Exodus
focuses on the construction of a god for personal use, Ezekiel portrays sin as an act of ingratitude toward God's gratuitous love.

As Pope Francis explains in the bull for the Jubilee of 2025,
"every sin 'leaves its mark.' Sin has consequences, not only out-
wardly in the effects of the wrong we do, but also inwardly, inas-
much as 'every sin, even venial, entails an unhealthy attachment
to creatures, which must be purified either here or on earth, or
after death, in the state called purgatory.' In our humanity, weak
and attracted to evil, certain residual effects of sin remain. These
are removed by the indulgence, always by the grace of Christ, who,
as Saint Paul VI wrote, 'is himself our indulgence.'"

Here, reflects the pope, "the mercy of God is stronger even
than this. It becomes *indulgence* on the part of the Father who,
through the Bride of Christ, his Church, reaches the pardoned sinner and frees him from every residue left by the consequences of
sin, enabling him to act with charity, to grow in love rather than
to fall back into sin. [...] Hence to live the indulgence of the Holy
Year means to approach the Father's mercy with the certainty that
his forgiveness extends to the entire life of the believer. To gain an
indulgence is to experience the holiness of the Church, who be-
stows upon us all the fruits of Christ's redemption, so that God's
love and forgiveness may extend everywhere."

Sin and Confession

In Judaism, a purification rite for sin existed long before Christianity in the liturgy of Yom Kippur, the Day of Atonement, which

is a solemn, annual ritual cleansing of the sins committed by the people. As described in the Old Testament, after the sacrifice of the victim and the sending of the scapegoat into the wilderness, the high priest would enter the Holy of Holies in the Temple of Jerusalem to sprinkle the *kapporet*, the cover of the Ark of the Covenant.

The Hebrew root of the words *kippur* (atonement) and *kapporet* (propitiatory) bear on the meaning of "to forgive" and "to cover," as the blood offered in sacrifice made God once again favorable toward the people and covered the sins committed by the Israelites over the previous year. This ritual then had to be repeated annually. By contrast, the sacrifice of Christ on the cross, which happened once and for all, efficaciously purifies the sins of all humanity—both present and future. This assurance is expressed in the Apostles' Creed, an ancient profession of faith that by the second century was definitively formulated to include the phrase: "I believe in the forgiveness of sins."

The certainty of forgiveness is linked, as the *Catechism of the Catholic Church* points out, "to faith in the Holy Spirit, but also to faith in the Church and in the communion of saints." Indeed, Christ bestowed the gift of the Holy Spirit upon the Apostles, directly associating this with the forgiveness of sins: "Receive the Holy Spirit. Whose sins you forgive are forgiven them, and whose sins you retain are retained" (John 20:22–23). These words indissolubly link God's action of forgiveness with what Catholic tradition calls the "power of the keys."

The *Catechism* clearly explains the duty and importance of frequently receiving the sacrament of penance, which offers all sinners "a new opportunity to convert and recover the grace of justification." Through this repeated experience of God's mercy, the faithful cultivate the desire to no longer offend God and to avoid occasions of sin. God's infinite love drives us to conversion, provoking a change of direction, and awakens the desire for good and the rejection of evil.

The sacrament of Reconciliation is a concrete and very real way to renew one's personal encounter with Jesus Christ. While it is often the culmination of a long personal journey involving inner struggle, many radical conversions also happen during the celebration of the sacrament itself. Here, supernatural grace—acting through the confessor—can work powerfully in the penitent's conscience, leading him in an instant to spiritual heights in a way natural criteria alone cannot explain.

This renewal always depends on two inseparable factors: the objective action of the Holy Spirit and the application of human freedom. Nowhere is this duality more fully realized than in the sacrament of Reconciliation, which is why the Church insists on the necessity of contrition for the validity of sacramental absolution.

Indeed, the necessity of contrition represents, in modern terms, the essential role of human freedom in embracing and renewing an encounter with Christ. Failing to require contrition would crush and humiliate human freedom, reducing the person within a mechanical view of human action—a view completely opposed to both the dignity of creation and our objective, everyday experience of existence.

The Remission of Sins

The first way in which sins are forgiven by the Holy Spirit is through baptism, as stated in the Creed recited at every Sunday Mass: "I confess one baptism for the forgiveness of sins." Jesus explicitly connects these elements: "Go into all the world and proclaim the Gospel to every creature. Whoever believes and is baptized will be saved, but whoever does not believe will be condemned" (Mark 16:15–16).

The other way the Holy Spirit forgives sins within the Church is through the sacrament of Reconciliation and penance. Often referred to as the "second penance," confession offers the ongoing purification that a Christian first receives on the day of baptism, typically as an infant, when one is reborn of water and the Spirit.

The remission of sins is an experience in faith of being forgiven by God, but it also involves clear doctrinal elements with moral, canonical, and pastoral implications. The theological foundation behind the faith in the remission of sins is rooted in the redemptive merit of Christ, and not in any human initiative, however praise-worthy. This is why sacramental confession is not merely a con-versation between a priest and the faithful; it is, rather, a renewal of the efficacy of Christ's sacrifice for a soul that, truly repentant, humbly seeks divine forgiveness.

An important aspect of the remission of sins is its ecclesial di-mension. Eight centuries ago, Saint Thomas Aquinas explained, "Just as in a living organism the activity of one member benefits the whole, something similar happens in the Mystical Body that is the Church. Among the truths of faith, the Apostles passed on to us the knowledge of the 'communion of saints,' which is the sharing of spiritual goods: the good accomplished by one person benefits the other faithful."

Aquinas continues: "It follows that, living in charity, each of us shares in even the smallest virtuous acts accomplished in the world. Through the communion of saints, the merits of Jesus are distributed to every faithful person, as are our personal merits." This means that the ecclesial nature of the remission of sins also integrates the forgiven person into a vast community, wherein a mysterious communion of spiritual goods abounds.

Entrusting the Church with the care for the "treasury of in-dulgences," God has desired to affirm that all who are redeemed by Christ are united in the *communio sanctorum* (communion of saints), which might be envisioned as a "covenant for salvation," or described more colorfully as a "spiritual bank of the Church." This treasure is continually enlarged by the infinite merits of Christ and the Blessed Virgin Mary, along with all the saints who already dwell in the fullness of paradise. The covenant is lived concretely by all the baptized who journey toward eternal salvation, whether still on earth or in purgatory undergoing purification for sins.

This is why every baptized person can gain an indulgence for herself or apply it to souls in purgatory. Those still living on earth possess the gift of freedom and can always deepen their conversions, whereas those in purgatory are assured *eventual* eternal salvation but no longer have the gift of freedom and cannot acquire further merits for themselves. However, the Church's mediation does not conflict with personal freedom, as those on earth cannot obtain an indulgence for another living person, that is, for someone who remains capable of personally accepting the gift of mercy for himself.

The Sacrament of Penance

Pope Francis emphasizes the fundamental importance of the sacrament of penance in relation to indulgences in the Jubilee Year: "The sacrament of penance assures us that God wipes away our sins. [...] The sacrament of Reconciliation is not only a magnificent spiritual gift, but also a decisive, essential and fundamental step on our journey of faith. There, we allow the Lord to erase our sins, to heal our hearts, to raise us up, to embrace us and to reveal to us his tender and compassionate countenance. There is no better way to know God than to let him reconcile us to himself and savor his forgiveness. Let us not neglect Confession, but rediscover the beauty of this sacrament of healing and joy, the beauty of God's forgiveness of our sins!"

The pope continues: "This experience of full forgiveness cannot fail to open our hearts and minds to the need to *forgive others* in turn. Forgiveness does not change the past; it cannot change what happened in the past, yet it can allow us to change the future and to live different lives, free of anger, animosity, and vindictiveness. Forgiveness makes possible a brighter future, which enables us to look at the past with different eyes, now more serene, albeit still bearing the trace of past tears."

The Rite of Penance, approved by Pope Paul VI in 1974, partitions this gesture into four stages. It begins with a reminder that the faithful who approach the sacrament "must first of all convert his heart to God. This inner conversion, which includes contrition for sin and the intention to lead a new life, is expressed by the sinner through confession to the Church, due compensation, and amendment of life. God grants the remission of sins through the Church, acting through the ministry of priests."

The initial step is contrition, which is "the sorrow and detestation of the sin committed, with the intention of sinning no more. We can only reach the Kingdom of Christ through *metanoia*— that deep and radical change when a person begins to think, judge, and reorder his life, motivated by the holiness and goodness of God as revealed to us and given in its fullness through His Son. The truth of penance depends on this contrition of heart. Conversion must engage the innermost being of a person, enlightening the spirit more and more and making him increasingly conformed to Christ."

The second, and essential, step is the confession of sins, which "comes from a true self-awareness and contrition for the sins committed. Both a thorough examination of conscience and the external confession must take place in the light of God's mercy. Confession requires the penitent to open his heart to the minister of God, and the minister, through the power of the keys to forgive or retain sins, pronounces a judgment *in persona Christi*."

This is followed by the completion of the conversion and involves "satisfaction, or compensations, for the sins committed— namely, the amendment of life and reparation for the damage caused. The type and extent of satisfaction should be suited to each individual penitent, so that one repairs the harm where he has erred and treats his sin with an effective remedy. The penance should truly be a remedy for sin and in some way transformative in one's life. The penitent, then, forgetting the past, enters with renewed commitment into the mystery of salvation and prepares for the future that lay ahead."

The penance given might be a prayer, meditation, a charitable act, or fasting. Prayer, almsgiving, and fasting were common practices in Jewish culture during Christ's time, and they should be rediscovered and valued today. Prayer is the act by which a person humbly places himself before the mystery of God—and without this there is no faith, spiritual life, or real possibility of conversion. Acts of charity, both material and spiritual, open the heart to others, whether they be the poor who need food and money for survival, or the wealthy who desperately need to rediscover life's true values. Fasting, especially in today's consumerist and indulgent society, educates us in a simplicity and sobriety of life that is essential only if for imagining an economy centered on humanity rather than profit.

At the end of confession, after receiving the priest's penance and before sacramental absolution, the penitent recites the Act of Contrition. The commonly used version is: "O my God, I am heartily sorry for having offended You, and I detest all my sins because I dread the loss of Heaven and the pains of Hell, but most of all because they offend You, my God, who are all good and deserving of all my love. I firmly resolve, with the help of Your grace, to confess my sins, to do penance, and to amend my life. Amen." There are also other penitential prayers, some drawn from the Psalms or Gospels, which can be recited according to personal preference or legitimate local customs, or used in preparation for confession. These might be as simple and heartfelt as, "Lord Jesus Christ, Son of God, have mercy on me, a sinner"; or "Cleanse me, Lord, of all my faults, cleanse me of my sins. I acknowledge my fault, my sin stands ever before me"; or "Have mercy on me, Oh Lord, in your mercy. Do not look upon my sins and erase my error. Create in me a pure heart and renew in me a spirit of strength and holiness."

Finally, absolution is given, which is the sign of divine forgiveness. "God uses visible signs to confer salvation upon us and to renew the broken covenant: all of this is part of the divine economy that led to the visible manifestation of God's goodness and His love for us. Through the sacrament of penance, the Father welcomes back the repentant son, Christ bears the lost sheep on His shoulders to return it to the fold, and the Holy Spirit sanctifies or intensifies His presence in the soul." The priest recites the absolution: "God, the Father of mercies, through the death and resurrection of His Son, has reconciled the world to Himself and sent the Holy Spirit among us for the forgiveness of sins; through the ministry of the Church, may God grant you pardon and peace, and I absolve you from your sins in the name of the Father, and of the Son, and of the Holy Spirit."

The Examination of Conscience

To make a good confession, it is necessary to prepare oneself by performing an examination of conscience in the light of God's word. This reflection should be grounded particularly in the Ten Commandments and the eight beatitudes from the Sermon on the Mount, as well as the moral teachings of the Gospels and the Letters of the Apostles.

The Ten Commandments are as follows: "1. You shall have no other gods before me. 2. You shall not take the name of the Lord your God in vain. 3. Remember to keep holy the Lord's Day. 4. Honor your father and your mother. 5. You shall not kill. 6. You shall not commit adultery. 7. You shall not steal. 8. You shall not bear false witness against your neighbor. 9. You shall not covet your neighbor's wife. 10. You shall not covet your neighbor's goods." To these, one adds Jesus' new commandment of love: "A new command I give you: Love one another. As I have loved you, so you must love one another." (John 13:34).

The eight beatitudes are found in the Gospel of Matthew, chapter 5: 1. Blessed are the poor in spirit, for theirs is the kingdom of heaven. 2. Blessed are those who mourn, for they shall be comforted. 3. Blessed are the meek, for they shall inherit the earth. 4. Blessed are those who hunger and thirst for righteousness, for they shall be filled. 5. Blessed are the merciful, for they shall obtain mercy. 6. Blessed are the pure in heart, for they shall see God. 7. Blessed are the peacemakers, for they shall be called children of God. 8. Blessed are those who are persecuted for righteousness' sake, for theirs is the kingdom of heaven.

The Church has established five further precepts, which the Catechism explains mean "to guarantee to the faithful the very necessary minimum in the spirit of prayer and moral effort, in the growth in love of God and neighbor."

The first is, "You shall attend Mass on Sunday and on holy days of obligation and rest from servile labor." It is an invitation to the faithful to sanctify the day on which we commemorate the resurrection of the Lord (Sunday) and all other feast days that are "obligatory" and recall the most sublime mysteries of the faith, the main events in the life of Our Lady, and the most important saints. Beyond participating in Mass, there is the call to devote this free time to acts that build up the interior life, personal relationships and friendships, and attention to those in particular need.

The second is, "You shall confess your sins at least once a year," which is a means of taking stock of one's spiritual state, taking responsibility for oneself and gauging the very sense of one's own life. This renders a person more worthy of receiving the Eucharist and more fruitfully.

The third is "receiving the sacrament of the Eucharist at least once per year at Easter." This emphasizes the significance of the

Easter celebration—that is, the fact that Christ through his Incarnation, passion, and death has saved us and opened before us the horizons of eternal happiness, in that paradise that is our ultimate destination.

The fourth is, "You shall observe the days of fasting and abstinence established by the Church." This is a requirement of a sobriety of life that every Christian must foster. This is not just abstinence from meat (for one can just as happily eat lobster!), rather training one's will to know how to live without something in a way that these acts can be offered up in love and self-denial to God as small mortifications.

The fifth is "taking care of the needs of the Church," which helps us feel as though we are truly members of the community and remain in solidarity with her. The fruits of this support are not only a benefit to the fundamental work of evangelization, but are also employed in the charitable works that diffuse the fragrance of Christ throughout the world.

An Outline for Meditation

In the *Rite of Penance*, there is also a useful general outline for the examination of conscience (and more recently, the Apostolic Penitentiary has suggested some additions, which are indicated here in italics). This outline initially suggests that the penitent examine himself regarding previous confessions, with the following three questions:

1. Do I approach the sacrament of penance with a sincere desire for purification, conversion, renewal of life, and a closer friendship with God, or do I rather consider it a burden that I am only rarely willing to undertake?
2. Have I forgotten or intentionally withheld serious sins in the previous confession or in past confessions?

3. Have I fulfilled the penance that was imposed on me? Have I repaired the wrongs I have done? Have I tried to put into practice the resolutions I made to amend my life according to the Gospel?

Then, three areas of personal examination are proposed in light of the word of God. The first is focused on the commandment: "You shall love the Lord your God with all your heart" (Deuteronomy 6:5):

1. Is my heart truly oriented toward God? Can I truly say that I love Him above all else, with the love of a child, by faithfully keeping His commandments? Do I let myself be too absorbed by worldly matters? Is my intention always pure when I act?
2. Is my faith in God strong, in He who has spoken to us through His Son? Have I fully adhered to the doctrine of the Church? Have I been concerned about my Christian formation, listening to God's word, participating in catechesis, and avoiding anything that might undermine my faith? Have I always professed my faith in God and the Church courageously and without fear? Have I shown myself to be a Christian in both my private and public life?
3. Have I prayed in the morning and at night? Is my prayer a true heart-to-heart conversation with God, or is it just an empty outward practice? Have I offered my work, joys, and sorrows to God? Do I turn to Him with trust even in times of temptation?
4. Do I show reverence and love for the holy name of God, or have I offended Him through blasphemy, false oaths, or taking His name in vain? Have I been disrespectful toward the Virgin Mary and the saints?
5. Do I sanctify the Lord's Day and Church feast days by actively, attentively, and devoutly participating in liturgical celebrations,

especially the Holy Mass? *Have I refrained from unnecessary work on holy days?* Have I observed the precepts of annual confession and Easter communion?

6. Are there "other gods" for me—things or interests in which I place more trust than in God, such as wealth, superstitions, spiritualism, or other forms of magic?

The second area of reflection is centered on the commandment, "Love one another as I have loved you" (John 15:12):

1. Do I truly love my neighbor, or do I exploit my brothers and sisters for my own interests and treat them in ways I would not want to be treated? Have I caused scandal through my words or actions?

2. In my family, have I contributed to the well-being and joy of others with patience and true love? For individual family members:

   For children: Have I been obedient, respectful, and honoring to my parents? Have I helped them in their spiritual and material needs? *Have I applied myself in school? Have I respected authorities? Have I set a good example in every situation?*
   For parents: Have I been concerned with the Christian education of my children? Have I set a good example? Have I supported and guided them with my authority?
   For spouses: Have I always been faithful in affection and actions? Have I been understanding in times of anxiety?

3. Do I share what I have, without selfishness, with those poorer than myself? Do I defend the oppressed and help those in need as far as I can? Or do I treat my neighbor with indifference or harshness, especially the poor, the weak, the elderly, the marginalized, and immigrants?

4. Do I recognize the mission entrusted to me? Have I participated

in the works of the apostolate and charity of the Church, and in the initiatives and life of my parish? Have I prayed and contributed to the needs of the Church and the world, such as for Church unity, the evangelization of peoples, and the establishment of justice and peace?

5. Do I care about the well-being and prosperity of the human community in which I live, or do I only care about my personal interests? Do I participate, as far as I can, in initiatives that promote justice, public morality, harmony, and charity? Have I fulfilled my civic duties? Have I regularly paid my taxes?

6. Am I fair, diligent, and honest in my work, eager to serve the common good? Have I paid my employees and subordinates fairly? Have I upheld contracts and kept my promises?

7. Have I given the legitimate authorities the obedience and respect that are due?

8. If I hold a position of authority or responsibility, do I only seek my own gain, or do I strive for the good of others, with a spirit of service?

9. Have I practiced truth and faithfulness, or have I harmed others through lies, slander, gossip, rash judgments, or in the violation of secrets?

10. Have I harmed the life and physical integrity of others? Have I offended their honor or damaged their possessions? Have I procured or advised abortion? *Have I remained silent when I could have encouraged good? In marital life, do I respect the Church's teaching on openness to life and its dignity? Have I acted against my physical integrity (e.g., sterilization)? Have I been faithful even in my thoughts?* Have I harbored hatred? Have I been quarrelsome? Have I used insults and offensive words, fostering disputes and resentment? Have I selfishly omitted testifying to the innocence of others? *While driving or using other means of transportation, have I endangered my life or the lives of others?*

11. Have I stolen? Have I unjustly desired the possessions of others? Have I harmed others in their respective property? Have I returned what I took and made restitution for the damages I caused?

12. If I have been wronged, have I shown a willingness to reconcile and forgive for the love of Christ, or do I harbor hatred and a desire for revenge in my heart?

The third area of reflection focuses on the call to "be perfect, as your heavenly Father is perfect" (Matthew 5:48):

1. What is the fundamental orientation of my life? Do I strengthen myself with the hope of eternal life? Have I tried to renew my spiritual life through prayer, reading, and meditating on the word of God, and participating in the sacraments? Have I practiced self-discipline? Have I been ready and determined to overcome vices, to control perverse passions and inclinations? Have I responded to feelings of envy and controlled my appetites? Have I been presumptuous and proud, asserting myself to the extent of undermining others and preferring myself over them? Have I imposed my will on others, trampling on their freedom and neglecting their rights?

2. How have I used my time, strength, and the gifts I have received from God, like the "talents of the Gospel"? Have I used all these means to grow daily in the perfection of spiritual life *and in service to others? Have I been lazy and inactive? How do I use the internet and other social media?*

3. Have I endured the pains and trials of life with patience *and in a spirit of faith*? How have I practiced self-denial, to complete what is lacking in the sufferings of Christ? Have I observed the law of fasting and abstinence?

4. Have I kept my body pure and chaste *according to my state of life*, remembering that it is a temple of the Holy Spirit, des-

tined for resurrection and glory? Have I guarded my senses and avoided contaminating my spirit and body with evil thoughts, desires, words, or actions? Have I indulged in reading, conversations, shows, or entertainment that conflict with human and Christian decency? Have I been a source of scandal to others through my behavior?

5. Have I acted against my conscience out of fear or hypocrisy?
6. Have I sought to live in the true freedom of the children of God, according to the law of the Spirit, or have I allowed myself to be enslaved by my passions?
7. *Have I omitted doing a good deed that was within my power to undertake?*

3

THE PILGRIMAGE
TO THE SEVEN CHURCHES

On the evening before Shrove Thursday in 1552, about 1,300 devout people gathered in front of Chiesa Nuova for the first procession organized by the founder of the Oratorian Fathers, the future Saint Philip Neri. He intended to revive the ancient tradition of pilgrimage to the tombs of martyrs and the most important places of worship in Rome. For many centuries prior, St. Peter's in Vatican City, St. John Lateran, St. Mary Major, St. Paul Outside the Walls, and St. Lawrence Outside the Walls—later joined by the basilicas of the Holy Cross in Jerusalem (Santa Croce in Gerusalemme in Rome) and St. Sebastian Outside the Walls—had been a constant destination for the faithful.

Traditionally, the first five basilicas were called "patriarchal," as each was associated with one of the patriarchates of the united Church before the Great Schism of 1054, which marked the separation between the Western Catholic Church and the Eastern Orthodox Church. These included the Patriarchate of the West (St. John Lateran), the Patriarchate of Constantinople (St. Peter's), the Patriarchate of Alexandria (St. Paul Outside the Walls), the Patriarchate of Antioch (St. Mary Major), and the Patriarchate of Jerusalem (St. Lawrence Outside the Walls).

An ancient and priceless testimony that highlights the deep devotion to the relics housed in these sacred places, even during the early Jubilees, is found in a letter that Francesco Petrarca wrote to Philippe de Vitry on February 15, 1350. He details the many marvels a pilgrim might witness in Rome:

> He will tread upon the thresholds of the Apostles, on earth soaked with the precious blood of martyrs. He will see the imprint of our Lord Jesus Christ on the Veronica cloth, displayed on the walls of all the temples. He will see the place where Christ appeared to Peter as he fled, leaving the imprint of his most holy feet on the hard stone for eternal adoration by mortals. He will enter the Holy of Holies, a place filled with heavenly grace. He will walk over the Vatican Hill and through the cemetery of Callixtus, filled with holy bones, and will see the manger and relics of the circumcised Jesus, and the vessel that preserves the purity of the Virgin's milk. He will gaze upon the ring of Agnes and proof of shameless intentions savagely realized. He will see the severed head of the Baptist, the gridiron of Lawrence, and the relics of Stephen, both content to rest united in one place. He will behold the fountains that sprang where Paul shed his blood in martyrdom, the spot where a stream of pure oil gushed into the Tiber at Christ's birth, the foundations of a magnificent temple marked by a miraculous snowfall in August, and the majestic walls of the ancient sanctuary that crumbled at the birth of the Virgin.

Philip Neri's idea was to replace the rowdiness of the circuses (that at the time involved Romans engaging in unruly and often obscene activities) with occasions of joyful prayer, with thoughts lingering on his motto, "vanity of vanities, all is vanity." Hymns like this were sung in unison, and participants shared food and moments of musical entertainment. To help the pilgrims derive the greatest spiritual benefit from a visit to the seven churches, the saint wrote nine guidelines, through these points of instruction urging them to "lift their minds to God, offering Him the sincerity of their hearts, with the intention of seeking only the glory of His Divine Majesty in all actions (and especially this), and intend to gain holy indulgences and to pray:

1. For the penance of sins;
2. For the correction of current lukewarmness, negligence, and other shortcomings in the service of His Divine Majesty;
3. In thanksgiving for the supreme blessing of having been delivered from so much misery and sin;
4. For the sanctity of our lord [the pope] and for the holy Church;
5. For all Christian prelates and princes;
6. For the Congregation of the Oratory (or the pious association to which one belongs) and for all religious orders;
7. For sinners who still wander in the darkness of a sinful life;
8. For the conversion of heretics, schismatics, and unbelievers;
9. For the holy souls in purgatory."

In a short time, the initiative gained increasing popularity, to the point where Pope Sixtus V, with the bull *Egregia populi romani pietas* on 13 February 1586, officially approved this pious practice since "these churches are renowned for their antiquity, for worship, for the venerable relics of martyrs, for the holy indulgences, and finally for the mystical significance of the number seven." He also worked to have roads built to make the journey between the basilicas more convenient. He elaborated on the symbolic meaning, noting the seven churches of Asia mentioned in Revelation as an example of the unity of the universal community, comparing them to the seven basilicas of Rome as a representation of the unity of the Catholic Church under the guidance of the pope. Many subsequent popes have recommended the continuation of this practice, and repeatedly enriched it with indulgences.

The walking route covers about 20 kilometers, undertaken in stages from St. Peter's to St. Paul Outside the Walls (6 kilometers), to St. Sebastian Outside the Walls (4 kilometers), to St. John Lateran (5 kilometers), to the Holy Cross in Jerusalem (1 kilometer), to St. Lawrence Outside the Walls (2 kilometers), and to St. Mary Major (2 kilometers). A charming testament to the difficulty this penitential journey entails can be found in the words of playwright Carlo Goldoni, who made the pilgrimage himself in the spring of 1759: "The discomfort and strain increase the merit […] / and in holy Rome, where open they lay hither / the treasures of Grace to the sinner, / for he who is intent on the sacred circuit/ who must travel fifteen miles and five hundred paces."

***

For ease of use, the simplified maps of the seven basilicas indicate only the main points of interest, with numbers in sequence corresponding to the descriptions and locations of artistic features. The information provided has been verified as of September 2024.

SAINT PETER IN THE VATICAN

Address: Piazza San Pietro
Internet site for the basilica: www.basilicasanpietro.va
Special Feasts: 22 February the Seat of San Peter is celebrated;
29 June is the solemnity of Saint Peter; 18 November the
anniversary of the dedication of this basilica is commemorated.
The basilica is open every day from 7 a.m. until 7 p.m.

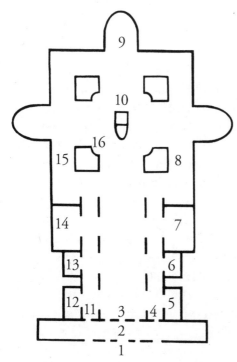

1 *Piazza and facade*
2 *Atrium*
3 *Central nave*
4 *Right nave*
5 *Chapel of the Pietà*
6 *Chapel of Saint Sebastian*
7 *Most Holy Sacrament Chapel*
8 *Gregorian Chapel*
9 *Apse*
10 *Cross of the transept*
11 *Left nave*
12 *Baptismal Font Chapel*
13 *Chapel of the Presentation of the Virgin*
14 *Chapel of the Choir and Sacristy*
15 *Clementine Chapel*
16 *Vatican Grotto*

This Catholic church, measuring nearly 187 meters in length and over 20,000 square meters in area, is the largest in the world. This is documented in the comparison with thirty other basilicas and cathedrals gauging the floors of the central naves. The construction of this monumental church was initiated by Emperor Constantine around 320 AD and consecrated in 326 by Pope Sylvester I at the time Christianity was made the state religion. It was built on the site traditionally believed to be the resting place of Saint Peter (the first pope) near Nero's Circus.

Originally, the church consisted of a rectangular hall, 90 meters long and 60 meters wide, and the edifice was modified and restored multiple times such that now it is composed of heterogeneous elements. In the mid-15th century, Pope Nicholas V decided to build a new, cohesive structure under the guidance of Leon Battista Alberti and Bernardo Rossellino, but this construction did not begin until 1505 under Pope Julius II.

The design was entrusted to Donato Bramante, who spent the following decade working on an ambitious plan, starting with the erection of the four central pillars to support the dome, counter pillars along the central nave and buttresses. Initially there was no clear markers for the final perimeter. Its perimeter was slowly built up over time (over a century and a half) as progress alternated with moments of crisis and stagnation. A succession of renowned architects were involved, including Raphael, Baldassare Peruzzi, Antonio da Sangallo, Michelangelo Buonarroti, Giacomo Della Porta, Domenico Fontana, Carlo Maderno, Gian Lorenzo Bernini, and Francesco Borromini. At long last, on 18 November 1626, Pope Urban VIII consecrated the new basilica, and under the papacy of Alexander VII (who died in 1667) the reconstruction was considered complete.

The subsequent work focused primarily on the interior decoration and the creation of funeral monuments, with contributions from countless artists. By the mid-18th century, evident cracks appeared on some of the walls and the large dome. This called for structural reinforcement, which was carried out by Luigi Vanvitelli. In 1834, Giuseppe Valadier made the summit more accessible, just before restoring the lanterns.

1. *Piazza and Façade*

The expansive piazza spreads out before the basilica, designed by Gian Lorenzo Bernini between 1656 and 1667. It is framed by two straight arms leading toward the façade and two semicircular colonnades with 284 marble columns arranged in four rows. Bernini asserted that the purpose was to "welcome the Catholics with open maternal arms, to confirm them in their belief, to re-unite heretics with the Church, and to illuminate the faith for non-believers." Travertine statues of 140 saints and martyrs, including 37 women, line the top of the colonnades. The central red granite obelisk, originally standing in Alexandria, Egypt, in 30 BC and transferred to Rome around 40 AD, is flanked by lions (the symbol of Pope Sixtus V) and eagles (the symbol of Pope Innocent XIII). The two fountains on either side are made of Chinese granite, and date back to Pope Innocent VIII (late 15th century, on the right) and Pope Clement X (late 17th century, on the left). At the foot of the picturesque staircase are the statues of Saint Peter (by Giuseppe De Fabris, on the left) and Saint Paul (by Adamo Tadolini, on the right), placed there by order of Pope Pius IX in 1847. Statues of the other eleven Apostles, along with Christ (in the center) and Saint John the Baptist (to his right), are located on the upper balustrade of the basilica. To the right of the basilica is the Apostolic Palace, where one sees a window at which the pope traditionally delivers the Sunday Angelus. On the corner is a mosaic copy of the 15th century icon "Our Lady, Mother of the Church" (the original is housed in the Colonna Chapel inside the basilica), commissioned by Pope John Paul II in a gesture of gratitude after surviving the assassination attempt on 13 May 1981. The majestic façade, clad in travertine and accented by Corinthian pilasters and columns, was completed between 1607 and 1614 under the direction of Carlo Maderno. It has five entrance portals to the atrium, each flanked by Ionic columns. Above the central portal is a 17th century marble bas-relief by Ambrogio Buonvicino, depicting "The Passing of the Keys." The dome, designed by Michelangelo and completed by Della Porta and Fontana, features an external drum nearly 60 meters in diameter and an ogival cupola (the cross at the top, on a bronze ball coated in gold, stands about 135 meters above ground level). The idea of building two bell towers to further frame the structure and enhance the verticality of the basilica was considered but ultimately abandoned due to the ground slowly giving way. For this reason, only the bases of the towers remain today, with wide arches crowned with mosaic clock faces, both designed by Valadier at the end of the 18th century. From the central loggia, the pope traditionally delivers the *Urbi et Orbi* blessing after his election and for the solemn blessings bestowed on the world at Easter and Christmas.

2. Atrium

Designed by Maderno and constructed between 1608 and 1612, the atrium features two vestibules where one views the equestrian monuments of Constantine (to the right, by Gian Lorenzo Bernini) and Charlemagne (to the left, by Agostino Cornacchini). The atrium is nearly 71 meters long, with a ceiling adorned with stucco depicting "Episodes from the Life of Saint Peter," and along the cornice are 38 statues of martyred popes from the early centuries. Five monumental doors lead into the basilica, beginning with the one on the far left, traditionally used for funeral processions and therefore called the "Door of Death." Completed by Giacomo Manzù in 1964, this door displays the "Assumption of Mary" on the left and the "Crucifixion of Jesus" on the right. Next is a more recent door by Luciano Minguzzi (1977), featuring twelve panels illustrating the themes of "Good" (on the right) and "Evil" (on the left). The central door, known as the "Filarete Door" (the nickname of the 15th century sculptor Antonio di Pietro Averlino), features larger images above, on the right showing Christ and the beheading of Saint Paul, and the Virgin Mary and the crucifixion of Saint Peter. Above this is a marble bas-relief by Bernini depicting Christ giving the keys to Saint Peter. Next to it is the door realized by Venanzo Crocetti in 1965, with the first relief illustrating the proclamation of the sacraments to humanity, and the others depicting each of these seven sacraments. Finally, on the far right is the Holy Door, commissioned by Pope Pius XII to Vico Consorti for the 1950 Jubilee. It has sixteen panels depicting biblical episodes, alongside the coats of arms of twenty-nine popes under whom Holy Years have been celebrated (with space remaining for seven more).

3. *Central Nave*

Immediately upon entering through the central doorway, one sees a large disc of red porphyry, marking the spot where medieval emperors knelt to be crowned by the pope. The two holy water fonts on each side, with marble angels holding yellow Sienese marble shell-shaped basins, date back to the Jubilee of 1725. The pillars are covered with multicolor marble and adorned with 56 medallions featuring the busts of popes, 104 doves with olive branches, and 192 angels. Altogether, 39 statues of founders and foundresses of religious orders are placed in upper and lower niches (another twenty statues are located on the outside), while 28 statues representing virtues are positioned along the entablature. On the farthest right-hand pilaster stands the famous bronze statue of Saint Peter seated on a marble throne (probably made by Arnolfo di Cambio in the 13th century), whose right foot is traditionally kissed or touched by pilgrims in devotion.

4. *Right Nave*

On the opposite façade, above the interior of the Holy Door, is a mosaic representation of "Saint Peter with the Keys" by Giovanni Battista Calandra, set against a gold background. On the left side, the monuments include Christina of Sweden (designed by Fontana in the late 1600s, with a bronze bust of the queen and a bas-relief of her solemn abjuration of Protestantism in 1654), Matilda of Canossa (completed by Bernini in 1644, depicting the countess as a protector of the papacy, holding the keys and the tiara on the left and the staff of command on the right, with a bas-relief depicting Emperor Henry IV's plea to Pope Gregory VII to lift his excommunication in 1077), Pope Gregory XIV (with a sarcophagus flanked by high-reliefs of "Religion" and "Justice," and above a 16th century icon, "Virgin Mother of the Pilgrims"). On the right side, the monuments include: Pope Leo XII (by Giuseppe De Fabris, 1836, featuring the pope giving his blessing, and allegories of "Religion" and "Justice," the latter holding a sword), Pope Innocent XII (by Ferdinando Fuga and Filippo della Valle, mid-18th century, depicting the pope on a throne between allegories of "Charity" and "Justice"), Pope Gregory XIII (by Camillo Rusconi, 1723, showing the pope giving a blessing between the allegories of "Religion" and "Magnificence," resting on an urn with a bas-relief of "The Approval of the Calendar Reform"). At the far end there is the altarpiece of Saint Jerome, featuring a mosaic entitled, "The Communion of Saint Jerome" (completed in 1732, based on a 1614 painting by Domenichino). Beneath it lies the body of Pope Saint John XXIII, whose face is covered by a wax mask.

5. *Chapel of the Pietà*

Since 1749, this chapel has housed a group of sculptures made from Carrara stone. Our Lady is depicted in a pyramidal three-dimensional composition, rendered symbolically as young as she was at the moment of the Incarnation, seated on a rock reminiscent of

Mount Calvary. With her left hand open, she appears to offer the lifeless body of Jesus—whom she holds in her arms and on her lap—to the world. Michelangelo completed this work in 1499 at the age of 24, under the commission of Cardinal Jean Bilhères de Lagraulas. It is the only work the artist ever signed (one can see it on the sash that falls from the Virgin's shoulder). The mosaics on the vestibule ceiling show angels tracing the sign of the cross on the foreheads of the saved.

6. *Chapel of Saint Sebastian*
The mosaic altarpiece, created by Pietro Paolo Cristofari in 1736, depicts the martyrdom of Saint Sebastian. Beneath the altar is the tomb of Pope Saint John Paul II. To the left, a bronze monument to Pope Pius XII (by Francesco Messina, 1965) shows the pope seated and imparting his blessing while holding the Sacred Scriptures. To the right, a gilded bronze statue of Pope Pius XI (by Francesco Nagni, 1964) portrays the pope as the bishop of Rome, wearing a miter on his head and on his cloak is a clasp adorned with a dove symbolizing the Holy Spirit.

7. *Chapel of the Blessed Sacrament*
The gilded bronze and lapis lazuli ciborium was designed by Bernini, who took inspiration from Bramante's *aedicule* (small shrine) at San Pietro in Montorio. The tabernacle is surrounded by twelve Corinthian columns and topped with small statues of Christ, the Apostles, and Saint Paul. On either side, two angels are depicted in prayer. The altarpiece depicting the Trinity was painted by Pietro da Cortona in 1632.

8. *Gregorian Chapel*
This corner space behind the supporting column of Saint Longinus was arranged by Della Porta under the commission of Pope Gregory XIII in 1578. The mosaics are inspired by Marian iconography, with

the Litany of Loreto depicted on the dome and other portraits of prophets and Doctors of the Church. The altar features the venerated icon Our Lady of Perpetual Help, a fragment of a 12th century fresco set in a multicolor marble frame, surrounded by eight gilded bronze angels. To the right is the monument to Pope Gregory XVI, with his arm outstretched in a blessing flanked by allegories of "Wisdom" and "Prudence." Moving straight ahead, on the right side is the 1769 monument to Pope Benedict XIV, showing the pope likewise giving a blessing, with "Wisdom" and "Disinterest" on either side. In the northern transept's semicircular space, the central altar is dedicated to Saints Processus and Martinian, prison guards who were converted and baptized by Saint Peter and later martyred. Behind the pilaster of Saint Helen is the monumental tomb of Pope Clement XIII, created by Canova in 1792. The pope is depicted kneeling in prayer, with allegories of "Religion" and the "Presence of Death" beside him. To the left is the Navicella (vessel) altar, with a 17th century mosaic by Cristofari (modeled after Giotto's early 14th century original) depicting Jesus with the Apostles in a boat tossed by the stormy Sea of Tiberias, a metaphor for the Church guided by the Lord through all her difficulties.

9. *Apse*

The apse contains the monumental structure designed by Bernini and completed in 1666 to house the *Cathedra Petri* (Chair of Saint Peter), believed to be the wooden seat of the first pope. A bas-relief on the back of the bronze throne shows Christ entrusting Peter with the Church, surrounded by statues of the Church Fathers from both Greek and Latin traditions (from left to right: Ambrose, Athanasius, John Chrysostom, and Augustine). Above, an alabaster oval window features a dove symbolizing the Holy Spirit, and is divided into twelve sections representing the Apostles. It is encircled by golden clouds and numerous angels. To the left of the apse stands a monument to Pope Paul III, commissioned by the pope himself in the mid-16th century and executed by Della Porta. The bronze statue of the pope stands atop a marble base and is flanked by statues of "Justice" and "Prudence". On the right, one finds the tomb of Pope Urban VIII, set by Bernini in 1647, which features a bronze statue of the pope enthroned, with the figure of "Death" seated on the marble sarcophagus and allegories of "Charity" and "Justice" on either side.

10. *Cross of the Transept*
At the center of the so-called "Octagon" stands Bernini's nearly 30-meter-high *baldacchino*, completed in 1635. The structure features four spiral marble columns decorated with vine motifs and a canopy adorned with angels and cherubs, all underneath a cross atop a golden globe. The canopy shelters the papal altar, a marble slab from the Forum of Nerva, consecrated in 1594 by Pope Clement VIII, and positioned directly above the traditional site of Saint Peter's tomb. Above it looms Michelangelo's dome, encircled by the Latin inscription from the Gospel of Matthew: *Tu es Petrus et super hanc petrum aedificabo ecclesiam meam et tibi dabo claves regni caelorum* ["You are Peter, and on this rock I will build my Church, and I will give you the keys of the kingdom of heaven" (Matthew 16:18–19)]. The sixteen sections of the dome feature mosaics by Cavalier d'Arpino from 1605, depicting multiple representations of God the Father, Christ, the Virgin Mary, angels, Apostles, saints, patriarchs, and bishops. The four large medallions at the corners show the busts and symbols of the four evangelists: Saint Matthew with the angel and Saint Mark with the lion (by Cesare Nebbia), Saint Luke with the ox and Saint John with the eagle (by Giovanni De' Vecchi). The dome is supported by four pillars, each with a colossal statue inaugurated in 1640: Saint Veronica holding the shroud of Christ (by Francesco Mochi), Saint Longinus with the spear that pierced Christ's side (by Bernini),

Saint Helen with the cross she discovered in Jerusalem (by Andrea Bolgi), and Saint Andrew with the X-shaped cross of his martyrdom (by François Duquesnoy). In front of the *baldacchino* the *Confessio* opens, aptly named to recall the heroic profession of faith by early Christian martyrs. This early 17th century work by Maderno sits directly above Saint Peter's tomb and features a double flight of sixteen steps illuminated by 89 bronze-gilded cornucopia lamps, designed by Mattia de Rossi. Preceding it are statues of Saints Peter and Paul by Biagio de' Giusti, installed in 1616. Behind them is the pallium niche, where a bronze urn holds these liturgical garments that are blessed by the pope each year on June 29 and given to metropolitan archbishops.

11. *Left Nave*
On the left side, several statues are displayed. These include the monument to Maria Clementina Sobieska (designed by Filippo Barigioni in 1745, on the sarcophagus one sees the figure of "Charity" by Pietro Bracci, and a mosaic of the Polish queen by Cristofari), a monument to Pius X (created in 1923 by Pier Enrico Astorri and Florestano Di Fausto), showing the statue of the canonized pope in papal attire, with bronze reliefs on the door depicting some of his initiatives. There is also the monument to Leo XI (erected in 1652 and designed by Alessandro Algardi), featuring a statue of the pope in papal vestments seated on the sarcophagus and surrounded by the allegories of "Magnanimity" and "Liberality." On the right side is the Stuart monument (a stele [slab] sculpted by Canova for three members of the English royal family), showing two mourning wraiths with torches turned upside down, flanking a symbolic door that leads to eternal life with God. Next is a monument in honor of Innocent VIII (created in 1497 by Antonio del Pollaiolo out of gilded bronze), featuring the pope lying on a sarcophagus below, and above a statue of his likeness bestowing a blessing, surrounded by bas-reliefs of the "Virtues". The monument to Innocent XI (cre-

ated in 1701 by Pierre-Étienne Monnot) shows the pope holding the papal tiara and keys in his left hand, with allegories of "Religion" and "Justice." The bas-relief on the pedestal depicts the liberation of Vienna from the Turkish siege in 1683. At the altar behind it is a mosaic copy of Raphael's *Transfiguration* (the original painting is housed in the Vatican *Pinacoteca*, or art gallery). Beneath the altar is the body of Blessed Pope Innocent XI.

12. *Baptismal Chapel*
A Roman porphyry basin was repurposed by Fontana in 1697 to create the Baptismal Font, gilded in bronze featuring two angels on either side and the *Agnus Dei* above. The walls are adorned with early 18th century mosaics, including the baptism of Christ in the center, Saint Peter baptizing his jailers (Processus and Martinian) on the left, and Saint Peter baptizing the centurion Cornelius on the right. The vestibule ceiling also features mosaics inspired by baptismal themes.

13. *Chapel of the Presentation of the Virgin Mary*
The mosaic altarpiece, created by Cristofari in 1728, depicts the "Presentation of the Child Mary at the Temple." Beneath the altar lies the tomb of Saint Pope Pius X. The monument on the left is dedicated to Pope Benedict XV (created by Pietro Canonica in 1928) and presents the pope in prayer, while the bronze relief behind this recalls his intense efforts during World War I when among other deeds he added an invocation to the Queen of Peace to the Litany of Loreto. The monument on the right honors Pope John XXIII, featuring a bronze bas-relief by Emilio Greco from 1967 that commemorates key moments of his papacy.

14. *Choir Chapel and Sacristy*
This chapel is enclosed by a curtain behind a bronze gate from 1760 when used during ceremonies of the Vatican Chapter. Its

altar features a 1747 mosaic of the Virgin and Saints John Chrysostom, Francis of Assisi, and Anthony of Padua, with a crown placed here by Pope Pius IX in 1854 after the proclamation of the dogma of the Immaculate Conception. On either side are the benches of the wooden choir stalls carved in 1626, depicting biblical episodes and sacred figures. Additional biblical scenes are featured in the gilded stucco reliefs on the ceiling, designed by Giovanni Battista Ricci in the early 17th century.

15. *Clementine Chapel*

Behind the statue of Saint Andrew lies the Clementine Chapel, designed by Michelangelo and later completed by Della Porta during the pontificate of Pope Clement VIII, who oversaw the decoration initiated in the mid-16th century by Pomarancio. The mosaics depict the dove of the Holy Spirit, angels with medallions, and Doctors of the Greek and Latin Churches. The altar is dedicated to Saint Gregory the Great, whose relics are kept here. The 1772 mosaic depicts a miracle of Saint Gregory. To the left side is the monument to Pius VII, completed in 1831 by Bertel Thorvaldsen, featuring the pope giving his blessing, flanked by small statues of "History" and "Time," and larger ones of "Divine Fortitude" and "Wisdom." Continuing straight ahead, on the left is the monument to Pius VIII, created in 1866 by Pietro Tenerani, showing the pope kneeling and accompanied by statues of Christ and the Apostles Peter and Paul. The door below leads to the sacristy, where a plaque lists the names of the 149 popes buried in the basilica. At the end of the accessible walkway there is a round room featuring a large marble floor crest of Pope Pius VI and a mosaic copy of Caravaggio's early 17th century painting, *The Entombment of Christ* (the original is displayed in the Vatican *Pinacoteca*). After passing the southern semi-circle transept (where the central altar is dedicated to Saint Joseph), behind the statue of Saint Andrew are: the monument to Alexander VII, completed by Bernini in

1678, with the pope kneeling in prayer, a winged bronze figure of "Death" at the center, and allegories of "Charity" and "Truth" below; the Colonna altar, featuring a 15th century icon of the Madonna and Child painted on a column taken from the old basilica; the altar of Saint Leo the Great, with a marble altarpiece from 1653 by Algardi, depicting Pope Leo's meeting with Attila in 452; the monument to Alexander VIII, featuring a bronze statue of the pope, designed by Angelo De Rossi, flanked by allegories of "Religion" and "Prudence."

16. *Vatican Grottos*

The current entrance to the Vatican Grottos is located at the statue of Saint Andrew, and here visitors quickly reach the central nave in front of the *Confessio*, which offers a view of the niche from behind containing the tomb of Saint Peter. Flanking the outer arch are 14th century sculptures from the monuments of Boniface VIII (with the two angels) and Urban VI (with the two lions). Behind is a 9th century mosaic, and extensively restored, depicting Christ in the act of blessing. On the opposite side of the nave, a statue sculpted by Canova portrays Pope Pius VI in a prayerful demeanor. In the first chapel to the left, there is a remarkable mid-15th century marble relief, the "Madonna and Child with Saints Peter and Paul" by Isaia Di Pisa. Continuing along the nave, visitors come across the tomb of Pope Benedict XVI (first niche on the left), featuring a late 15th century marble relief of the "Madonna and Child with Two Angels" by Giovanni Dalmata. Nearby is the tomb of Blessed Pope John Paul I (third arch on the right), whose sarcophagus features two 15th century bas-reliefs of praying angels by Andrea Bregno. The tomb of Saint Pope Paul VI (fourth niche on the left) displays fragments of 15th century reliefs on the back wall. To the left, after the Gallery of Clement VIII (where at the beginning, on the left side, one can see a 5th century mosaic fragment of the head of Saint Peter), there are the niches containing the sarcophagi with the reclining figure of Pope Paul II, a late 15th century work by Mino da Fiesole. There is also Pope Nicholas V, whose monument was originally located in the old basilica, as well as Pope Boniface VIII, sculpted by Arnolfo di Cambio at the start of the 14th century. On the right-hand wall at the beginning of the exit corridor is a Renaissance marble tabernacle, with a 14th century fresco, "The Virgin of Sorrows," by Lippo Memmi. Not far from this, visitors will see the sarcophagus with the reclining figure of Pope Callixtus III, accompanied by 15th century marble bas-reliefs on the wall. Finally, near the exit on the left side, stands the statue of Saint Peter *in cattedra*, and a 2nd or 3rd century Roman philosopher figure to which, during the medieval period, a left hand holding a key was added along with a new head and a remodeled right arm.

SAINT JOHN LATERAN

Address: Piazza di Porta San Giovanni
Official website of the basilica: www.vatican.va/various/basiliche/
san–giovanni/index_en.htm
Official website of the shrine: www.scala-santa.com
Feasts: On 9 November the anniversary of the dedication of the
basilica is commemorated; on 27 December the feast of St. John
the Evangelist is celebrated; the birth (24 June) and memorial
of the martyrdom (29 August) of John the Baptist are celebrated
here as well.

The basilica is open every day from 7 a.m. until 6:30 p.m.
The shrine of the Holy Stairs is open from 7 a.m. until 1:30 p.m.
and from 3 p.m. until 6:30 p.m.

1 *Façade and Portico*
2. *Central Nave*
3 *Corsini Chapel*
4 *Santori Chapel*
5 *Lancellotti Chapel*
6 *Cloister*
7 *Altar of the Most Holy*
   Sacrament
8 *Papal Altar and Apse*
9 *Massimo Chapel*
10 *Torlonia Chapel*
11 *Fresco of Boniface*
   VIII
12 *Lateran Baptistry*
13 *Loggia of the Blessing*
14 *Shrine of the Holy*
   Stairs

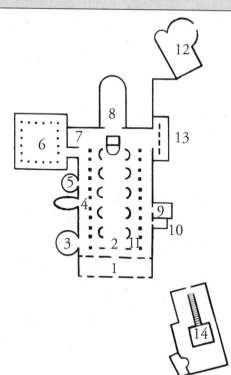

For seventeen centuries, this church has been the cathedral of the Diocese of Rome and thus bears the title *Omnium urbis et orbis ecclesiarum mater et caput* ("Mother and head of all the churches of the city [of Rome] and of the world"), as inscribed in Latin on its façade. In fact, from the 4th to the 14th century, this basilica served as the primary residence of the popes before they moved to Avignon, the Quirinal, and later the Vatican (with numerous other temporary relocations along the way).

The basilica was built on land donated to the Church by Emperor Constantine and was consecrated by Pope Sylvester I in 324, dedicated to the Most Holy Savior, whose image is visible in the ancient mosaic high on the façade and in the statue from 1735 high above it all. Later, the titles of two other saints were added—Saint John the Baptist (in the 9th century by Pope Sergius III, depicted in the statue on the left holding a staff ending in a cross) and Saint John the Evangelist (in the 12th century by Pope Lucius II, depicted in the statue on the right holding a chalice from which, according to tradition, he drank poison and survived).

The original Constantinian structure had a layout similar to the current one, with five naves and perimeter walls roughly matching what we see present-day. At the end of the 13th century, Pope Boniface VIII undertook major renovation work, including the construction of a new loggia for blessings and frescoes by Cimabue and Giotto. Unfortunately, these latter works and other priceless art and liturgical furnishings that once adorned the basilica during its first millennium have been lost due to barbarian raids, fires, and negligence, especially during the time the popes remained in France (1309–1377).

Following the return of Pope Gregory XI to Rome, several partial restorations were undertaken, but it wasn't until the late 16th to mid-17th centuries that the entire area was fully restructured. Between 1586 and 1589, on the remains of this ancient patriarchy, the Lateran Palace was built to the right of the basilica by

Domenico Fontana, which now serves as the headquarters of the Vicariate of Rome. In 1600, Giacomo Della Porta redesigned the transept, and between 1650 and 1660 Francesco Borromini reconstructed the central nave with five large arches on either side and massive pilasters that incorporated the more ancient columns.

1. Façade and Portico

In 1735, the 12th century brick façade was replaced with the current travertine material by architect Alessandro Galilei, featuring a portico with architraves, a loggia with arches, a central tympanum, and a balustrade crowned with statues, including the three titular figures of the basilica and twelve saints. The bronze door knockers on the main entrance, originally from the *Curia Hostilia* in the Roman Forum (where the Senate met until 52 BC), were transferred here in 1660 by Pope Alexander VII. The door on the far right is the Holy Door: the one currently in place is made of bronze and designed by Floriano Bodini for the Jubilee Year of 2000. On the opposite side stands a marble statue of Emperor Constantine, sculpted around 320.

2. Central Nave

The central nave is 130 meters long and has a Cosmatesque floor commissioned by Pope Martin V in 1426, and a gilded wooden ceiling designed by Pirro Ligorio and carved by Flaminio Boulanger, which was requested by Pope Pius IV in 1562. In the early 18th century, monumental statues of the Apostles were placed in niches prepared by Borromini, above which are stucco reliefs (1648–49) depicting scenes from the Old Testament (on the left) and the New Testament (on the right). Oil paintings of prophets adorn the walls, rendered by various artists. Behind each Apostle there is a marble door symbolizing the heavenly Jerusalem, which as described in the Book of Revelation, "is encircled by great and high walls with twelve gates."

3. *Corsini Chapel*

Built simultaneously with the new façade by Alessandro Galilei, this chapel is dedicated to the 14th century Florentine saint, Andrew Corsini, depicted in a mosaic on the altar based on a painting by Guido Reni. It was commissioned by Pope Clement XII to honor his illustrious ancestor. A bronze statue of the pope by Giovanni Battista Maini stands in the monument on the left, featuring an urn and columns made of porphyry taken from the Pantheon.

4. *Santori Chapel*

This was founded at the end of the 16th century by Cardinal Giulio Antonio Santori, whose tomb is located on the left side with a bust sculpted by Girolamo Finelli. On the altar, there is a marble crucifix on a gilded bronze cross (of unknown origin), and below it is "Our Lady of Grace" from the school of Perugino.

5. *Lancellotti Chapel*

Built at the end of the 16th century by Cardinal Scipione Lancellotti, the chapel was restored at the end of the 17th century, with stucco added in the vault by Filippo Carcani. The oval painting on the altar, depicting the stigmata of Saint Francis, is by Giovan Battista Puccetti, while the marble "Pietà" on the right wall was sculpted by Antonio Montauti.

6. *Cloister*

Built in the early 13th century by the Roman marble workers of the Vassalletto family, the cloister is considered a masterpiece of the dawn of Gothic architecture in Europe. The small, coupled columns (some decorated with mosaics) support the arches. The rich entablature, with its numerous bas-reliefs and figures, is stunning. Along the walls, there are various works of art, including 12th century bronze door knockers (by Pietro and Uberto da Piacenza), the 13th century funeral monument of Riccardo Annibaldi (by Arnolfo di Cambio) and contemporary altar and ciborium of Mary Magdalen (by Deodato di Cosma). Historically noteworthy is the inscription of Pope Gregory XI's 1372 bull proclaiming the primacy of the Lateran Basilica.

7. *Altar of the Most Holy Sacrament*

Four ancient bronze columns support a triangular golden metal tympanum featuring a painting of God the Father by Pomarancio from the late 16th century. Enclosed is the contemporary tabernacle, designed by Pompeo Targone. Above it is an 18th century silver bas-relief of the Last Supper by Curzio Vanni, which replaced the original that was melted down in 1797 to pay tribute to Napoleon. According to tradition, the relic of the table used at the Last Supper is kept here. Opposite the altar is a giant organ built by Luca Biagi in 1598, with columns bearing foliage engravings by Giovanni Battista Montano.

8. *Papal Altar and Apse*

At the end of the central nave and under the giant arch one finds the papal altar, historically reserved for use by the pope. It was restored in 1851 and contains the wooden table on which all popes up to Saint Sylvester I (who died in 335) are said to have celebrated Mass. The ciborium overhead, erected in 1367 after the previous one was destroyed in a fire, holds 19th century silver reliquaries of the heads of Saints Peter and Paul. The *baldachino*'s eight statues date back to 14th century reconstruction, whereas the twelve frescoes were added in the late 15th century. At the base of the altar, in the expanded 1853 area of the *confessio*, is the burial place of Pope Martin V, with a bronze tomb slab from 1443 attributed to Simone Ghini. The new apse, designed by Francesco Vespignani and inaugurated by Pope Leo XIII in 1886, replaced the original 1291 mosaic by Jacopo Torriti and Jacopo da Camerino, which was demolished when the apse was pushed farther back. The current mosaic, a faithful copy created in 1883–84, depicts: at the top, Christ in bust form surrounded by angels; beneath, a cross with Our Lady encrusted with gems, Saints Peter and Paul and others on a hill top that is heavenly Jerusalem, from which extend four streams (the Gospels), at which drink deer and sheep; and, finally, nine of the Apostles. At the base is the papal *cathedra* that dates back to the late 13th century, symbolizing Christ's victory over the devil, represented by the four animals at its base that harkens back to Psalm 91: "You will tread on the lion and the adder; the young lion and the serpent you will trample underfoot."

9. *Massimo Chapel*

This chapel was designed in the late 16th century by Giacomo Della Porta, who also created the tomb of Domenico Massimo (on the left). The oil painting on the altar is of the Crucifixion and was painted by Sermoneta in 1575.

10. *Torlonia Chapel*

Built in the mid-19th century by Quintiliano Raimondi for the princes of the House of Torlonia, this was the last family chapel to be added to any of the Roman basilicas. On the altar is a marble rendering of Christ's deposition by Pietro Tenerani, with a malachite and lapis lazuli frontal piece from Russia. The tomb of Giovanni Torlonia (on the right) features allegorical statues representing "Charity" and "Commerce," and the tomb of Anna Schultheiss Torlonia (on the left) and features "Goodness."

11. *Fresco of Boniface VIII*

Attributed to either Giotto or Pietro Cavallini, this is the only remaining fragment of the fresco originally located in the *Loggia delle Benedizioni* (Blessings Loggia) and was moved to the basilica in 1786. According to tradition, and indicated by the Latin inscription below it, this fresco depicts Pope Boniface VIII in 1300 announcing the first Jubilee in history. Another hypothesis suggests this dates back to 1297 and portrays the pope's coming to take possession of the Lateran on 23 January 1295. On the next pillar is the cenotaph for Pope Sylvester II, whose ancient marble slab is called the "sweating stone," as it is said to become moist and creaky when the death of a pope approaches.

12. *Lateran Baptistery*

Located to the right of the basilica, the *San Giovanni in Fonte* [Saint John at the Font] baptistery is the oldest in all of Christianity, built during the reign of Constantine. According to tradition, Constantine was baptized here by Pope Sylvester. The double order of columns, porphyry below and white marble above, surrounds a green basalt urn used in much earlier periods for the full immersion baptism of catechumens. Each of the four chapels houses priceless art: the Chapel of the Baptist features bronze doors from the Baths of Caracalla; the Chapel of Saint Rufina has a 5th century mosaic; the Chapel of Saint Venantius features 7th century mosaics and a 16th century wooden ceiling; and the Chapel of Saint John the Evangelist contains bronze door knockers dating back to 1196.

13. *Blessings Loggia*

Constructed by Domenico Fontana in 1586 by order of Pope Sixtus V, this *loggia* replaced a 12th century portico, the same period that brought two three-lancet bell towers. These have been restored multiple times. The bronze statue, created in 1608 by Nicolas Cordier, represents King Henry IV of France, who donated the revenues from Clairac Abbey to the Lateran Capitol. In the piazza in front of the basilica, an Egyptian obelisk made of red granite dating to the 15th century BC was installed in 1588. It is the tallest obelisk in Rome, standing at 31 meters (plus an additional 16 meters for the base), and bears the inscription: "Constantine, victorious through the intercession of the Cross / baptized by Saint Sylvester in this place / propagated the glory of the Cross."

14. *Shrine of the Holy Stairs*
In 1589, Domenico Fontana designed this building using the same architectural style as the *Loggia*, at the behest of Pope Sixtus V who wanted to incorporate the Oratory of San Lorenzo in Palatio, an ancient private chapel of the popes. Of the five staircases that branch out from the atrium, the central one is traditionally considered the staircase from Pilate's Praetorium, which Jesus ascended on Good Friday. This *Scala Santa* [Holy Stairs] consists of 28 veined marble steps that the faithful climb on their knees as an act of devotion and penance. It is believed that traces of the Redeemer's blood remain on the 2nd, 11th, and 28th steps. The walls feature 28 frescoes depicting the Passion of Christ, culminating in the crucifixion, all painted by Cesare Nebbia in 1590. Below the fresco of the crucifixion, a grate allows a glimpse into the *Sancta Sanctorum* [Holy of Holies], where an inscription in Latin reads, "There is no holier place in all the world." The altar within the *Sancta Sanctorum* houses sacred relics, including an *acheiropoieta* image of Christ (that is, an image not made by human hands but happened miraculously), his sandals, a fragment of the true Cross, and the head of the martyr Saint Praxedes. The presbytery's ceiling features a 13th century mosaic of Christ Pantocrator ("Almighty"), while the cross-vaulted ceiling and lunettes display contemporary frescoes portraying the four evangelists and scenes from the lives of various saints. To the right of the building stands the so-called Leonian Triclinium, an apse-shaped niche with a mosaic depicting Christ surrounded by eleven Apostles, a 1743 replica of the original medieval piece, now protected by a railing added by Pope Pius XI in 1933.

SAINT PAUL OUTSIDE THE WALLS

Address: Piazzale San Paolo
Website of the basilica: www.basilicasanpaolo.org
Feasts: On 29 June the solemnity of St. Paul is observed; 18 November is the commemoration of the dedication of the basilica.
The basilica is open every day from 7 a.m. until 6:30 p.m.

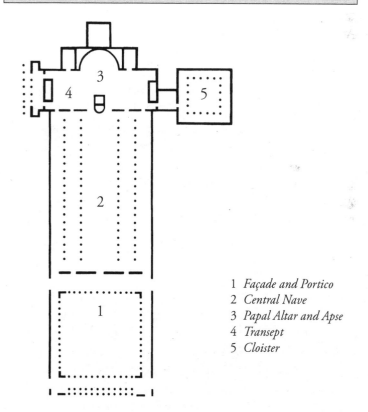

1 *Façade and Portico*
2 *Central Nave*
3 *Papal Altar and Apse*
4 *Transept*
5 *Cloister*

Dedicated to Paul, known as the "Apostle of the Gentiles" because his mission focused particularly on non-Jewish peoples (so-called "Gentiles"), this basilica was initiated around 324 by Emperor Constantine on the exact location of the saint's burial in 67 AD after his martyrdom by decapitation in the nearby area of *Acque Salvie* (now known as *Tre Fontane*, named for the tradition of the three fountains that miraculously sprang up where his head bounced). Born in Tarsus in Cilicia (modern-day Turkey) around 4 AD, Saul (as he was known then) was one of the fiercest persecutors of early Christian communities until his famous conversion on the road to Damascus. He was later arrested in Rome during Nero's persecution of Christians.

Several decades later, under Emperor Theodosius and the august Valentinian II and Arcadius, the church was significantly expanded, making it about nine times larger than the previous structure and its orientation was changed from east to west where the land was a good deal flatter. However, the focal point of Paul's tomb remained unaltered.

Pope Siricius consecrated the basilica in 390, and devotion to St. Paul turned the area into a cemetery that housed approximately 5,000 grave sites between the 4th and 6th centuries. These tombs belonged to devotees who wished to be buried near the Apostle, as indicated by inscriptions visible until 1823. In that year, on the night of July 15–16, a fire nearly destroyed the entire complex. Pope Leo XII's appointed commission decided to rebuild the basilica with the same layout and dimensions as before, and the work took about 30 years. The new basilica was inaugurated by Pope Pius IX on 10 December 1854.

One of the historical and artistic particularities of this basilica is the series of round mosaic papal portraits. Originally painted as frescoes (41 of which are preserved in the Vatican *Pinacoteca*), the series began under Pope Leo I around the year 450 and was restored after the fire. The portraits after being restored started with

St. Peter (at the top right of the apse) and continue up to the present day, including 273 popes, among them three non-existent popes and eight anti-popes (who were considered legitimate at the time). Contrary to popular belief, there is still space for future popes—even after Pope Francis, six round spaces remain in the right nave, with an additional 20 spaces available at the beginning and end of the outer naves.

1. *Façade and Portico*

The monumental four-sided portico, surrounded by white granite columns, contains in its center a statue of St. Paul, finished in 1850 by Giuseppe Obici. The statue holds a sword that symbolizes his martyrdom, and a book that represents the letters he wrote to guide the faithful. This space was once where catechumens (those preparing for baptism) would wait while the Eucharist was celebrated, as they were allowed to participate only in the first part of the Sunday liturgy (the liturgy of the Word that precedes the liturgy of the Eucharist). The mosaics on the façade, designed by Filippo Agricola and Nicola Consoni, depict Christ flanked by Peter and Paul (at the top), the Lamb of God from which the source of salvation flows (in the middle), with the mystical cities of Jerusalem and Bethlehem on either side. Below them are the prophets Isaiah, Jeremiah, Ezekiel, and Daniel. The central bronze portal, crafted by Antonio Maraini around 1930, depicts episodes from the lives of Saints Peter and Paul, with the busts of the Apostles within a cross (vertical axis) together with symbols of the evangelists (horizontal axis). The Holy Door, located to the right and crafted by Enrico Manfrini out of bronze for the Jubilee Year 2000, exhibits various scenes, including Paul's journey to Damascus, Christ's Resurrection, and Pentecost. The interior side retains the remarkable Byzantine door cast in Constantinople in 1070, which features 54 bronze panels illustrating biblical scenes and characters. At the back of the basilica on the side of the apse, the composite bell tower, designed by Luigi Poletti in the mid-19th century, has a square base for the first three stories but becomes octagonal for the fourth, and ends in a circular *tempietto* with Corinthian columns on the topmost level.

2. *Central Nave*

The central nave is lined with twenty monolithic columns of Montorfano granite on each side (with an additional twenty columns forming the five-nave interior of the basilica). The coffered golden ceiling, which was restored in the 16th century style after the fire, features the coat of arms of Pope Pius IX at its center. Above, and continuing into the transept, a series of thirty-six frescoes, painted in 1857, depict key events from the life of St. Paul. The ancient, original stained-glass windows were replaced with thin slabs of alabaster. At the end of the nave stands the triumphal arch erected by Emperor Theodosius in 386, adorned with a mosaic restored in 1853 showing Christ surrounded by symbols of the four evangelists, and below this are the twenty-four elders from the Book of Revelation. On the back side of the arch is a medallion-shaped image of Christ giving his blessing, with remnants of the original 13th century mosaic created by Pietro Cavallini for the old façade. At the base of the arch are statues of St. Peter (left) by Ignazio Jacometti, and St. Paul (right) by Salvatore Revelli, with the statues of the other Apostles, sculpted by various artists, appearing in niches along the side walls.

3. *Papal Altar and Apse*

The earliest reference to St. Paul's burial on the Via Ostiense comes from Eusebius of Caesarea's *Historia ecclesiastica* (completed in 325). Since 2007, visitors can view the rough marble sarcophagus of the Apostle through a grate beneath the papal altar (along with a display of the chains from his imprisonment). Beneath the glass floor lies the ancient apse from Constantine's original basilica. The altar is surmounted by a Gothic ciborium created by Arnolfo di Cambio in 1285, supported by four porphyry columns with gilded *capitelli* (tops). In the corner recesses are statues of Saints Peter, Paul, Timothy (Paul's faithful disciple), and Benedict (founder of the monastic order that still cares for the basilica). To the right is an imposing Paschal candle stand that is over five meters tall, carved in 1170 by Pietro Vassalletto and Nicolò D'Angelo, featuring scenes from the Passion and Resurrection, alongside variations of human, animal, and foliage motifs. The majestic 13th century mosaic in the apse (covering nearly 300 square meters) has been restored multiple times. It depicts Christ Pantocrator, with his right hand raised in a gesture signifying his dual nature (both divine and human) and the Holy Trinity. Surrounding him are Luke and Paul (left), and Peter and Andrew (right). Below them are Barnabas, Thaddeus, James the Greater, Matthew, Philip, John, two angels with a gem-encrusted cross at their center, James the Lesser, Bartholomew, Thomas, Simon, Matthias, and Mark (from left to right). At the feet of Jesus is a small figure of Pope Honorius III, who commissioned the work. The papal chair at the back of the apse, designed by Poletti and made of marble and gilded bronze, features a relief depicting Christ's endowment of the keys to Peter, realized by Pietro Tenerani.

4. Transept

On the left side of the transept, a portico designed by Poletti (commissioned by Pope Gregory XVI) leads one outside. This portico reuses twelve Greek marble columns that were previously housed inside the old basilica. The altars on both sides of the transept are wrapped in malachite and lapis lazuli, gifts from Tsar Nicholas I in the mid-19th century. On the left, there is a rendering of the conversion of St. Paul painted by Vincenzo Camuccini, flanked by statues of Pope Gregory the Great and St. Romuald. On the opposite side, a mosaic reproduction of the Assumption of the Virgin

Mary stands between statues of St. Benedict and St. Scholastica, designed by Giulio Romano. The chapel on the left side of the apse holds the Blessed Sacrament and displays a 13th century polychrome wooden crucifix attributed to Cavallini. According to tradition, this crucifix spoke to St. Bridget of Sweden in 1350 (a statue of her can be found in the left corner, sculpted by Stefano Maderno). The chapel also contains a 13th century mosaic icon of the Mother of God, before which St. Ignatius of Loyola and his companions took their vows as Jesuits on 22 April 1541. On the right side, the Chapel of St. Lawrence contains a 15th century marble triptych attributed to the school of Andrea Bregno, with 19th century inlaid choir stalls on either side.

5. *Cloister*
The cloister, built in the early 13th century by Nicola and Pietro Vassalletto, features paired columns in a variety of styles supporting arches that are adorned with mosaics and marble inlays. Among the artifacts displayed here are the Sarcophagus of the Muses from the 3rd–4th century, used in 1128 as the tomb of Pietro di Leone, and a marble statue of Pope Boniface IX, sculpted by an unknown Roman artist at the end of the 14th century.

SAINT MARY MAJOR

Address: Piazza di Santa Maria Maggiore
Website: www.basilicasantamariamaggiore.va
Feasts: On the last Sunday of January the anniversary of the translation of the icon of Our Lady *Salus Populi Romani* is commemorated; On 5 August, the memorial of Our Lady of the Snows, the anniversary of the dedication of the basilica is celebrated.
The basilica is open every day from 7 a.m. until 7 p.m.

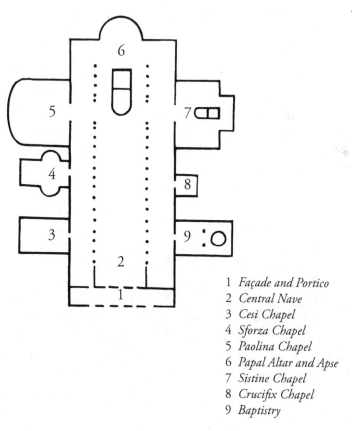

1 *Façade and Portico*
2 *Central Nave*
3 *Cesi Chapel*
4 *Sforza Chapel*
5 *Paolina Chapel*
6 *Papal Altar and Apse*
7 *Sistine Chapel*
8 *Crucifix Chapel*
9 *Baptistry*

The origin of this basilica stems from an ancient tradition concerning a dream Pope Liberius had on the night between August 4th and 5th, in the year 358. In the dream, the Virgin Mary asked him to build a church at the location where despite the summer heat he would find a patch of snow. The following morning, the pope discovered the summit of the Esquiline Hill covered in snow. There he marked the perimeter of the first church in the world dedicated in its name to the Virgin Mary, and he did so with a stick on the fresh snow.

Nothing remains of that original structure, known then as the Liberiana Basilica. However, there are more concrete traces of the later Sistine Basilica, inaugurated by Pope Sixtus III a few years after the Council of Ephesus in 431, which proclaimed the dogma of Mary the most holy Mother of God. At the beginning of the 9th century, the papal altar was raised, and a *confessio* (a shrine or space for relics) was built beneath it just as in St. Peter's. A more radical restructuring took place in 1288 under Pope Nicholas IV, especially with the addition of the transept.

Between the 14th and 15th centuries the bell tower was erected, which at 75 meters is the highest in Rome. For the Jubilee of 1575, Pope Gregory XIII modified the street today called Via Merulana to connect it with St. John Lateran. Pope Paul V later reorganized the square in front of the basilica in the early 17th century, placing a Corinthian column (from the Basilica of Maxentius) in the center, crowned with a bronze statue of Our Lady by Guillaume Berthelot and a fountain designed by Carlo Maderno. In the mid-18th century, architect Ferdinando Fuga aligned the pillars and columns of the naves with the side chapels.

In 1825, Pope Leo XII commissioned architect Giuseppe Valadier to consolidate the mosaics, and in 1916 Pope Benedict XV restored the coffered ceiling. In the late 19th century, the piazza in the rear underwent the last round of modifications—which required lowering the street level—where Pope Sixtus V had previously installed a Roman obelisk (an Egyptian imitation transported from the Mausoleum of Augustus), and where Pope Clement IX had commissioned Carlo Rainaldi in 1669 to design the grand staircase leading to the basilica.

1. Façade and Portico

The two-tiered façade, designed with five openings on the lower level and three arches on the upper level, is crowned by a marble statue of the Madonna and Child by Giuseppe Lironi. It was completed by Ferdinando Fuga, who had set it in front of the preexisting 13th century structure. Inside the portico one finds the bronze statue of Philip IV of Spain sculpted by Girolamo Lucenti in 1692 along with scenes from the life of the Our Lady rendered in 1947 by Lodovico Pogliaghi. The Holy Door to the left was made by Luigi Enzo Mattei in 2001. A staircase on the left leads to the *loggia*, where the ancient mosaics by Filippo Rusuti are visible, depicting Christ enthroned and four scenes from the basilica's founding.

2. Central Nave

The central nave, 85 meters long, is separated from the side naves by twenty monolithic columns on each side, topped with ionic *capitelli* that support the entablature, which is decorated with a 5th century mosaic frieze. The coffered wooden ceiling, with 105 panels, is said to have been gilded with the first gold brought from the Americas, donated by Philip IV and Isabella of Spain. The central row of coffers displays the coat of arms of Pope Alexander VI and the Borgia family crest featuring a bull. The Cosmatesque flooring, dating back to the 12th century, is partially intact. Below each of the 36 windows are 5th century mosaic panels (nine of which were replaced with paintings in 1593 due to deterioration) depicting the stories of Abraham and Jacob (on the left side) and Moses and Joshua (on the right side).

3. *Cesi Chapel*

Commissioned in the mid-16th century by Cardinal Federico Cesi to architect Guidetto Guidetti, this chapel was decorated by Sermoneta with frescoes of prophets, sibyls, and angels. The tombs of the cardinals and brothers Federico (on the right) and Paolo Cesi (on the left) were designed by Giacomo Della Porta, and feature bronze statues of the deceased lying on marble sarcophagi. The chapel is dedicated to St. Catherine of Alexandria, whose life is depicted in mid-17th century paintings by Giovanni Angelo Canini. The altarpiece, illustrating her martyrdom by decapitation, was painted by Sermoneta.

4. *Sforza Chapel*

Designed by Michelangelo around 1560 for Cardinal Guido Sforza, this chapel was built by architects Tiberio Calcagni and Giacomo Della Porta. Della Porta is credited with the tombs of the two brothers, Guido (on the right) and Alessandro Sforza (on the left), which feature oil portraits of the deceased and black marble sepulchers. The altarpiece, depicting the coronation of Our Lady, is by Cesare Nebbia.

5. *Pauline Chapel*

This chapel was designed in 1605 by architect Flaminio Ponzio, under the commission of Pope Paul V, to house the icon of Our Lady *Salus Populi Romani* (Salvation of the Roman People), which tradition holds was painted by St. Luke the Evangelist on a plank of cedarwood. The icon is kept above a monumental altar adorned with precious gems (agates, amethysts, jaspers, and lapis lazuli), designed by Girolamo Rainaldi and executed by Pompeo Targone, with a decorative frieze of angels sculpted by Camillo Mariani. A bas-relief by Stefano Maderno above shows Pope Liberius tracing the basilica's perimeter in the snow. Many artists, all coordinated by the Cavaliere d'Arpino (Giuseppe Cesari, who is responsible for the prophets in the dome and the frescoes around the altar), contributed to its overall decoration. The dome's fresco of the Virgin with the twelve Apostles is by Cigoli, while the lunettes and arch frescoes on both sides, particularly those featuring the saints, are by Guido Reni. The tombs of Popes Clement VIII (right) and Paul V (left) are adorned with statues sculpted by Silla da Viggiù.

6. *Papal Altar and Apse*

The triumphal arch is the only remaining element of the 5th century apse, featuring the inscription *Xystus episcopus plebi deus* (Sixtus [III], bishop of the people of God). Above it, Saints Peter and Paul are depicted, centered around a symbolic representation of Christ's second coming according to the Book of Revelation, whereas the other mosaics focus on the infancy of Christ. The mosaics on the far side of the apse, completed in 1295 by Jacopo Torriti, feature Jesus crowning his Mother, both seated on a gem-encrusted throne, surrounded by angels, and in the band below this are five scenes from Mary's life. The papal altar was designed by Ferdinando Fuga and includes a porphyry urn supported by bronze angels sculpted by Filippo Tofani, topped by a wooden *baldachino,* or canopy, featuring the symbol of the Holy Spirit. Giuseppe Valadier added gilded bronze leaves to the structure in 1823. On the floor to the right side of the altar is the tomb of Gian Lorenzo Bernini and his family. Beneath the altar is the *confessio,* constructed by Virginio Vespignani (who used over a dozen different kinds of marble) and inaugurated by Pope Pius IX in 1864. The statue was commissioned by his successor, Leo XIII, to Ignazio Jacometti. The urn in the niche, a priceless artifact by Valadier made of gold, silver, and rock crystal, contains relics of wood from what is traditionally believed to be the manger of baby Jesus and thus thousands of years old.

7. *Sistine Chapel*

Commissioned by Pope Sixtus V, the Sistine Chapel was designed in 1584 by architect Domenico Fontana. It incorporated the ancient oratory desired by Pope Sixtus III in 432, which included a replica of the Bethlehem grotto, and Arnolfo di Cambio's nativity scene, sculpted in Carrara marble around 1290 under Nicholas IV. The statues of St. Joseph, the three Magi, the ox, and the donkey are original, whereas the Madonna and child Jesus are later additions during the 16th century. The chapel, which features a Greek cross plan with a large central dome and two smaller corollary chapels, was once the largest chapel in Rome. The magnificent gilded bronze tabernacle designed by Lodovico del Duca, featuring four life-size angels by Sebastiano Torrigiani, houses the Blessed Sacrament. The chapel's walls are decorated with frescoes coordinated by Cesare Nebbia and Giovanni Guerra, and depict episodes from the life of Mary and the infancy of Christ. The right side of the chapel houses the tomb of Pope Sixtus V (the statue is by Valsoldo), and the left side holds the tomb of Pope Pius V (the statue is by Leonardo Sormani).

8. *Chapel of the Crucifix*
Renovated for the Jubilee of 1750 by Ferdinando Fuga, this chapel is adorned with marble and ten porphyry columns. It houses various relics, including those of the martyrs St. Thomas Becket and St. Bibiana. The altar features a wooden crucifix from the first half of the 15th century, mounted on a flat porphyry cross.

9. Baptistery
Originally built by Ponzio in the early 17th century as a winter choir for the basilica's canons, this structure was converted two centuries later into the baptistery of the basilica. Giuseppe Valadier designed the baptistery, incorporating a porphyry basin and an arresting statue of St. John the Baptist. The marble altarpiece, depicting the Assumption of Our Lady, was sculpted by Pietro Bernini, the father of Gian Lorenzo Bernini, around 1610. On the ceiling, also from the same period, is a rendering of the Immaculate Conception, with Our Lady surrounded by prophets and Doctors of the Church, painted by Passignano.

SAINT LAWRENCE OUTSIDE THE WALLS

Address: Piazzale San Lorenzo
Basilca website: www.cappucciniimmacolata.it/roma-verano
Feasts: On 10 August the memorial of Saint Lawrence is observed.
The basilica is open every day from 7:30 a.m. until 12:00 p.m. and from 4:00 p.m. until 7:00 p.m.

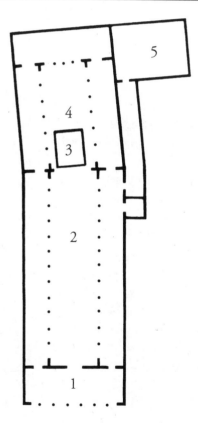

1 *Facade and Portico*
2 *Honorian Chapel*
3 *Crypt*
4 *Pelagian Basilica*
5 *Cloister*

"Lawrence was able with the faith alone to conquer the whip, the flame, torture, and the chains," writes Pope Damasus in his elegy in verse in honor of the saint a century after his martyrdom, which occurred on 10 August 258 AD under the persecution of Emperor Valerian. According to tradition, the saint—who was among the seven deacons of the Christian community and thereby entrusted with the apostolate of charitable works—responded to the request issued by a Roman prefect, Cornelius Secolare, who demanded Lawrence present him with the treasure kept in his care. Lawrence arrived surrounded by the poor: "Behold the stars and diamonds of the Church." As punishment, he was condemned to torture and laid on a grill over flames. He was buried in that same place in the catacombs of Ciriaca.

The early Constantinian basilica was rendered unstable due to landslides and water damage, and was reconstructed in the year 580 under the commission of Pope Pelagius II to rebuild directly over the tomb of the martyr, leveling the slope over the ancient sepulcher. Pope Clement II, around 1190 fortified the complex with the city wall and created a small village called *Laurenziopoli*, whose bell tower that is still visible on the right was once one of its defense towers. Later modifications were undertaken in the first half of the 1200s when Popes Honorius III and Innocent IV were inclined toward expansion. The floor of the basilica was raised so as to make room for a crypt, the previous central nave was made into the presbytery of the new building, and this latter space was elongated without maintaining the precise alignment of the axes.

The large piazza in front, where the granite columns stand tall and are crowned with the bronze statue of St. Lawrence, was finished in 1704 through the work of architect Alessandro Gaulli. The bombing of 19 July 1943 during World War II caused terrible damage to the basilica (in addition to the destruction of the surrounding village and three thousand casualties). The restoration was completed in only five years and used the original materials.

Yet the walls and the façade had to be stylized in a completely different manner given the irreparable harm done. Beginning in the early 1500s, the pastoral care of the basilica was entrusted to the Benedictines, who were replaced by canons regular of the Lateran in the 1600s, and then again by the Capuchins in the 1800s (who continue in that role today).

1. *Façade and Portico*
The façade features six marble columns with Ionic *capitelli* that support an entablature adorned with a frieze of porphyry discs and mosaic fragments. These lead to a sloped roof portico, constructed in the early 13th century by the Vassalletto workshop. Above the portico, there is a brick front with three windows. The entrance is flanked by stone lions from the 13th century, and two sarcophagi, the one on the left depicting scenes of the harvest (6th century) and the one on the right depicting biblical episodes (4th century). The walls of the portico are adorned with late 13th century frescoes depicting scenes from the lives of St. Stephen and St. Lawrence (on the left and right of the backdrop).

2. *Basilica of Honorius*
The basilica, divided into three naves by two rows of eleven columns made of various types of marble, has a Cosmatesque floor from the 13th century and a ceiling with wooden trusses. The funeral monument on the counter-façade, to the right of the entrance, is dedicated to Cardinal Guglielmo Fieschi. His marble sarcophagus, dating back to the 3rd century, features an incredibly detailed relief of a wedding ceremony. Halfway through the basilica, two ambos and a Paschal candelabra were also created by the Roman Cosmati workshop in the 13th century. On the right wall in the nave, fragments of frescoes from the mid-8th century depict the Madonna with the Child Jesus and saints, and another with Saints Lawrence, Andrew, and two others. The funeral monument

to Marquis Giuseppe Rondinini commemorates his death on 13 September 1649, during the Battle of Candia (modern-day Crete) between the Venetian Republic and the Ottoman Empire. The monument includes a striking copy of Medusa's head, reminiscent of Bernini's work, and a mosaic portrait of the marquis. Of all the 19th century frescoes by Cesare Fracassini that once adorned the central nave, only the Madonna with the Child Jesus among angels and saints on the triumphal arch and St. Stephen's ordination as deacon on the counter-façade remain. At the far end of the lateral naves, the underground Chapel of St. Cyriaca contains the 17th century tombs of Girolamo Aleardi and Bernardo Guglielmi (left), while the Chapel of St. Tarcisius (right), designed by Virginio Vespignani, features 17th century oil on canvas images that include images of St. Cyriaca burying St. Lawrence by Emilio Savonanzi (on the altar) and the beheading of St. John the Baptist by Giovanni Serodine (on the left).

3. *Crypt*

At the center of the stairs leading to the presbytery is the *confessio*, decorated in the early 17th century under Cardinal Francesco Boncompagni and later arranged in the mid-19th century by Virginio Vespignani. This area contains the tomb of St. Lawrence, which also houses the relics of St. Stephen and St. Justin. Behind the tomb, a marble slab upon which St. Lawrence was reportedly laid after his martyrdom is framed on the wall. According to ancient tradition, the saint's body left an imprint on the slab, as recorded by an inscription that unfortunately is now lost.

4. *Pelagian Basilica*

The presbytery is defined by ten columns, topped with an entablature adorned with tokens of weapons and leaves, and a matroneum with variegated columns above it. The central feature is a ciborium from 1148, created by the sons of Pietro Romano, made of four porphyry columns and covered with a pyramidal artifice. The 13th century Cosmatesque mosaic floor is preserved here. On this side the triumphal arch is decorated with a 6th century mosaic depicting Christ giving his blessing, flanked by St. Peter and St. Lawrence and Pope Pelagius II holding a model of the church (to the left), and St. Paul, St. Stephen, and St. Hippolytus (to the right). At the back of the presbytery is a Cosmatesque episcopal chair dating back to 1254, made of marble and mosaic, featuring geometric designs. In the rear, one finds the funerary chapel of Pope Pius IX done by Raffaele Cattaneo in the late 19th century, with mosaic depictions of saints and scenes from the pope's life designed by Ludovico Seitz.

5. *Cloister*
Accessible through the 19th century sacristy, the cloister was commissioned by Pope Clement III in the late 12th century and built by the Cosmati family. In the mid-13th century, a two-story *loggia* was added—the lower level features both single and paired columns, while the upper level has polifore windows from the 15th century. Displayed along the walls are numerous epigraphs from both pagan and paleo-Christian eras, along with fragments of sarcophagi and Roman and medieval bas-reliefs.

HOLY CROSS IN JERUSALEM

Address: Piazza di Santa Croce in Gerusalemme
Website: www.santacroceroma.it
Feastdays: On 20 March the anniversary of the dedication of the basilica is commemorated; on 18 August the feast of St. Helen is celebrated; on 3 May and 14 September the feasts of the discovery of the Cross and the exaltation of the Cross are celebrated, respectively.
The basilica is open on Saturday, Sunday, and the dates listed above and other days of holy obligation from 7:30 a.m. until 7:30 p.m. On all other days the hours are 8:00 a.m. until 12:45 p.m. and 3:30 until 7:30 p.m.

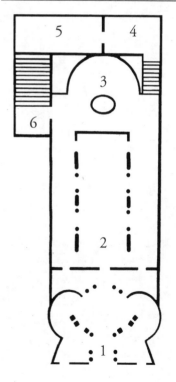

1 *Façade and Atrium*
2 *Central Nave*
3 *Papal Altar and Apse*
4 *Chapel of St. Helen*
5 *Chapel of St. Gregory*
6 *Chapel of the Relics*

This is the oldest devotional church in Rome, originally called only *Hierusalem* (the addition of *Santa Croce* dates back to the year 1003), and was founded by Helen, the mother of Emperor Constantine, around 330 after she returned from her pilgrimage to Palestine in 326. According to tradition, she did not just visit the holy sites of Jesus's life, but also undertook the mission of recovering some of the instruments of the Passion, which she brought back to Rome and kept in a palatial hall within her residence at the *Sessorium* (which, in Latin, refers to the imperial seat, built on the slopes of the Esquiline Hill sometime between the 2nd and 3rd centuries by Septimius Severus and Elagabalus). Evidence that this was not merely a private chapel but a place of worship for the faithful is corroborated by the discovery during archaeological excavations in the late 1990s of the remains of a baptismal font beneath the cubiculum (or private chamber) of Saint Helen. In confirmation of its importance, the pope had been celebrating the Good Friday liturgy here since the 5th century.

Shortly before the year 1000, Pope Benedict VII had a monastery built next to it, which through the years housed the Benedictines, the canons regular of Saint Fridianus, the Carthusians, and the Cistercians (since 2009 the parish has been overseen by diocesan clergy). In the 12th century, Pope Lucius II gave what had until then been essentially the ancient church (periodically renovated to provide the necessary liturgical areas) the make-over of a Romanesque basilica divided into three naves with a true façade, a bell tower, and a cloister.

In the 15th century, a new ceiling was installed, and vaults were constructed in the side naves. The placement of the semi-subterranean chapels and the addition of side altars are attributed to Cardinal Bernardino López de Carvajal, the titular patriarch of Jerusalem. Finally, in the mid-18th century, Pope Benedict XIV undertook significant renovations, and approved the design by architects Domenico Gregorini and Pietro Passalacqua, who replaced the medieval portico with a protruding oval-shaped Baroque atrium, and replaced the 15th century ceiling in the central nave with a wooden barrel vault.

1. *Façade and Atrium*

The captivating travertine façade features a single order of Corinthian pilasters, with a tympanum topped with a balustrade that holds statues of two angels in the center, and statues of the four evangelists, with St. Helena (on the left) and Constantine (on the right). In the background, the medieval brick bell tower with paired bifora windows stand out. The atrium, which displays columns from the ancient vestibule, consists of a central area and an elliptical walking path.

2. *Central Nave*

There are six granite columns on each side, with two incorporated in the pilasters, which separate the central nave from the side naves. The ceiling is adorned with stucco, and at its center is an 18th century painting by Corrado Giaquinto depicting the Virgin presenting St. Helen and Emperor Constantine to the Trinity. The ancient Cosmatesque floor was restored in 1933 for the Jubilee Year of Redemption. The two marble holy water fonts near the entrance, adorned with reliefs of fish (a symbol of Christ) and serpents (symbolizing the devil in flight), date back to the 15th century.

3. *Papal Altar and Apse*

In the mid-18th century, the medieval ciborium was replaced by the current *baldachino*, which at one time retained the original columns but now has a marble canopy topped with gilded bronze angels. The apparition of the Cross by Giaquinto decorates the ceiling. Beneath the main altar, in a black basalt basin adorned with lion heads and bronze lion feet, rest the bodies of the martyrs Saints Caesarius and Anastasius. In the semi-dome of the apse, a late 15th century fresco by Antoniazzo Romano illustrates the discovery of the true Cross (below) and Christ in glory (above), following the narrative of the *Legenda Aurea* by Jacobus de Voragine. It was commissioned by Cardinal de Carvajal, whose tomb is located to the left of the monumental tomb of Cardinal Francisco de los Ángeles Quiñones, established in 1536 by Jacopo Sansovino. This tomb, flanked by four columns (two in porphyry and two in *portasanta* marble), features a bronze tabernacle designed by Carlo Maderno, surrounded by marble sculptures of two angels (below), King Solomon (on the left), and King David (on the right).

4. *Chapel of Saint Helen*

Dating back to the time of Constantine, the chapel's ceiling features a mosaic created in the early 16th century by Baldassarre Peruzzi, depicting Christ giving his blessing, surrounded by the evangelists and four stories of the true Cross—including the curious appearance of a parrot that symbolizes the recently discovered Americas. The contemporary frescoes, also illustrating stories of the true Cross, were painted by Pomarancio. The statue of St. Helen is a replica by Giunone Barberini (the 2nd century statue is now housed in the Vatican Museums), with its head and arms refashioned and a cross added. The relics of the Passion were venerated here until 1570, when they were moved to a room above the monastery and later placed in the current shrine.

5. *Chapel of Saint Gregory*

Adjacent to the Chapel of Saint Helen, this chapel was built in 1520 when commissioned by Cardinal Carvajal. The bas-relief on the altar, depicting the *Pietà* in white marble against a black background, is the work of an unknown early 17th century sculptor. In the corridor is the tomb of Cardinal Joachim Besozzi, a Cistercian, designed by Innocenzo Spinazzi in 1755.

6. *Chapel of the Relics*

The chapel is reached after ascending a staircase whose walls are adorned with fourteen groups of bronze images depicting the Passion, all created by Giovanni Nicolini. It was designed by architect Florestano Di Fausto to replace the old sacristy, and inaugurated in 1930 but completed only in 1952, with stained glass windows by Cesare Picchiarini and mosaics by Corrado Mezzana. Inside the climate-controlled display case are six precious reliquaries, which replaced the older ones confiscated by the Roman Republic in 1798. From left to right at the top are: part of the finger of the Apostle Saint Thomas (a reminder of his doubt in the Gospel of John); the fragments from the grotto of Bethlehem, the Holy Sepulcher, and the column of the flagellation; and two thorns from the crown placed on Jesus' head at Pilate's praetorium. In the center: a gilded silver reliquary by Giuseppe Valadier (with a central medallion featuring a gold bas-relief of the Trinity, the Virgin of Sorrows below, and the Crucifixion of Christ and the two thieves at the bottom) that incorporates three fragments of the true Cross found on Golgotha by Saint Helen; Next to it on the left is the *patibulum*, the horizontal beam of the cross of the "good thief." At the bottom, from left to right: one of the three nails of the crucifixion (the others are said to be part of the Iron Crown in Monza Cathedral and the Holy Nail in Milan's *Duomo*) and the tablet of the *Titulus* whereupon Pilate inscribed "Jesus of Nazareth, King of the Jews" in Hebrew, Greek, and Latin. To the right is a full-size replica of the Shroud of Turin and the Shroud crucifix, a three-dimensional reconstruction of Jesus on the cross with all the wounds of the Passion, created by Monsignor Giulio Ricci.

SAINT SEBASTIAN OUTSIDE THE WALLS

Address: Via Appia Antica 136
Website: www.sansebastianofuorilemura.org
Feastdays: On 20 January the memorial of Saint Sebastian is celebrated.
The basilica is open every day from 7 a.m. until 6:30 a.m. (from March through October) and from 8 a.m. until 5:30 (from November through February).

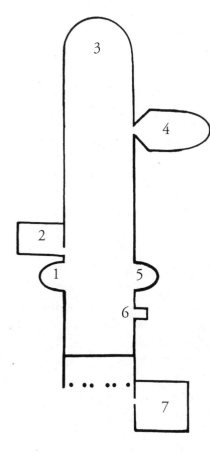

1 *Chapel of Saint Sebastian*
2 *Crucifix by St. Philip*
3 *Main Altar*
4 *Albani Chapel*
5 *Chapel of the Relics*
6 *Marble Bust of the Savior*
7 *Entrance to the Catacombs*

According to tradition, Saint Sebastian was an officer of Italo-French origins serving in the Praetorian Guard in Rome. During the anti-Christian persecution under Emperor Diocletian (which began with his rise to power in 284), Sebastian suffered martyrdom. He was first pierced with arrows and then, after miraculously recovering, he was beaten to death. The earliest records of him are found in the *Depositio martyrum* (mid-4th century), which commemorates him liturgically on January 20th, while more details about his death come from the *Acta sancti Sebastiani* from the 5th century. After some back and forth movements during the medieval period, his remains were placed here in 1218, while his head is kept in the Roman basilica of Santi Quattro Coronati.

Devotion to him grew quickly, particularly after he was named *defensor Ecclesiae* (defender of the Church) by Pope Caius at the end of the 3rd century, making him the third patron saint of Rome. However, it was only after 680, when his intercession was credited with ending a plague in Rome following a procession with his relics, that this basilica was named after him. Before that, the basilica was dedicated to the *Memoria apostolorum*—that is, in memorial of the co-patrons Peter and Paul, who were traditionally believed to have been buried here until the 3rd century, when St. Peter was moved to the Vatican hill and St. Paul to Via Ostiense.

Construction of the basilica began in the first half of the 4th century, featuring a central hall with two side naves that surround the apse, and it has received partial modifications over time. Between 1608 and 1612, Cardinal Scipione Borghese funded the rebuilding efforts led by architects Flaminio Ponzio and Giovanni Vasanzio who gave the church its current form. The new design utilized only the central nave of the old basilica. Its ornate wooden coffered ceiling is adorned with a relief figure of Saint Sebastian and the coats of arms of Cardinal Borghese and Pope Gregory XVI (who restored it in the mid-19th century). The façade was enhanced with a portico featuring three arches supported by paired granite columns taken from the original building, and the small square in front was modified so as to connect it with the street.

1. *Chapel of St. Sebastian*

Commissioned in 1672 by Cardinal Francesco Barberini, this chapel features marble adornments executed by the artist Ciro Ferri. The altar contains the urn with the remains of St. Sebastian, which were previously located in the ancient altar of the crypt in the catacombs below. The statue of the saint, created by the sculptor Giuseppe Giorgetti based on a design by Bernini, depicts Sebastian pierced by the arrows of his martyrdom.

2. *Crucifix of St. Philip*

This polychrome wooden crucifix is believed to have spoken to St. Philip Neri. Created between the 14th and 15th centuries, its 1964 restoration revealed traces of the symbols of the evangelists at the four ends of the cross.

3. *Main Altar*

Designed by Ponzio, the high altar is flanked by four ancient green marble columns and features Innocenzo Tacconi's painting, *The Crucifixion of Christ with the Madonna and St. John the Evangelist* (1609–14). At each side in the apse are the busts of the Apostles Peter and Paul, sculpted by Nicolas Cordier in 1608.

4. *Albani Chapel*

Pope Clement XI (Giovanni Francesco Albani, pope from 1700 to 1721) had this chapel built as his family's burial chapel. Dedicated to the 3rd century pope and martyr St. Fabian, who was once co-patron of the basilica, it was constructed between 1706 and 1712 with the design by architect Carlo Fontana. The chapel is adorned with polychrome marble and a priceless bronze and iron gate dating back to 1714. The statue of St. Fabian is the work of sculptor Pietro Papaleo.

5. Chapel of the Relics

Completed in 1627 by Duke Maximilian of Bavaria during the restoration commissioned by Cardinal Borghese, this chapel displays one of the arrows that pierced St. Sebastian, the column to which he was bound during his martyrdom, the head of St. Callistus, and a stone linked to the apocryphal *Acts of Peter*. This stone is allegedly involved in the episode where Peter, fleeing persecution under Emperor Nero around 63–64 AD, encounters Christ on the Appian Way and asks, "*Domine, quo vadis?*" ("Lord, where are you going?"). Christ's responds that he is going to Rome to be crucified again, and this compels Peter to return and face his own martyrdom. A church was built on this site, mentioned in a bull of Pope Gregory VII in 1074, but the stone from this location, believed to bear the footprints of Christ, is displayed in this chapel of the basilica.

6. Marble Bust of the Savior

This was the last work of Gian Lorenzo Bernini, sculpted for private devotion in 1679, a year before his death. The bust was rediscovered only in 2001 in the convent attached to the basilica. According to scholar Daniela Di Sarra, the face of Christ in this sculpture was inspired by Bernini's vision of the Shroud of Turin, which he had seen during his stay in Turin in May of 1665.

7. Entrance to the Catacombs (for opening hours, ticket prices, and other information pertaining to planning one's visit, see www.catacombe.org)

Between the 1st and 4th centuries, this area at the third mile of the Appian Way located outside the Aurelian Walls served as the site of numerous pagan and later Christian burials. The name *katà kumbas* (Greek for "near the cavities") referred to the depressions formed by pozzolana quarries. This term evolved into *ad catacumbas* in Latin, eventually becoming the general term for Christian burial sites in Rome. Near the entrance, visitors can see a small slab known as the "tombstone of symbols" featuring the Christogram, which looks like an anchor (symbolizing faith in the resurrection) and a fish (in Greek, *iktùs*, an acronym for "Jesus Christ Son of God Savior") combined. In the crypt of St. Sebastian, the remains of the ancient altar base and a marble bust of the martyr attributed to Bernini are on display. The *Piazzuola* area houses three 2nd century mausoleums carved into tuff rock, still bearing visible frescoes and stucco. In the *Triclia* area, numerous inscriptions and "graffiti" from the 3rd and 4th centuries have been left by devotees, some invoking the Apostles Peter and Paul. According to tradition, the Apostles lived here for a time and were temporarily buried here during Emperor Valerian's persecution (257–258).

4

THE HISTORY OF THE JUBILEE YEARS

1300: The First Christian Jubilee

The tradition of Holy Years in Rome began, one could say, "by popular demand." As the end of 1299 approached, none of the members of the papal court had yet considered organizing a specific liturgical-pastoral event. However, a spontaneous gathering of the faithful had flocked to St. Peter's on the evening of December 24 (the last day of the year according to Vatican custom at the time) to urge Pope Boniface VIII to convene the College of Cardinals to decide whether or not to grant their request for an extraordinary "pardon."

Cardinal Jacopo Caetani degli Stefaneschi recorded the testimony of a 107-year-old man, who was summoned before the pope and recounted how "his father had brought him to Rome to obtain an indulgence in the previous centenary year (1200), living on very little food and warned by his own father because he didn't think the son would survive to see the next centenary year."

Although no confirmation of this account was found in the records of the Apostolic Chancery, nevertheless the persistence of the faithful—who had begun to arrive from outside Rome as well—led Boniface to issue the bull *Antiquorum habet* on February 22, 1300 (the feast of the Chair of St. Peter), officially establishing the Jubilee of the "centenary year."

The pope specified that pilgrims must visit the basilicas dedicated to St. Peter and St. Paul, stipulating that "Romans must do so for thirty consecutive or non-consecutive days, at least once a day, and foreigners or pilgrims for fifteen days in the same manner. However, everyone will merit more and gain the indulgence more effectively if one visits these basilicas more frequently and devoutly." An estimated two million people took part in the Jubilee.

Pilgrims were encouraged to chant three communal verses: *Annus centus, Romae semper est Iubileus. Crimina laxantur, cui poenitet ista donantur. Hoc declaravit Bonifacius et roboravit.* ("Centenary year, in Rome it's ever the Jubilee. Who repents of sin is gifted. This is declared and decreed by Boniface.") Additionally, a catchy tune became popular: *Sempre a Roma, ogni cent'anni, / c'è la gioia senza affanni; / dei peccati e dei malanni / si perdonano e i danni, / se nel cuore e nel pensiero / tu ti penti per davvero. / Bonifacio dichiarò / questo e poi lo confermò.* ("In Rome every hundred years, there is joy with no worry; sins and troubles forgiven and healed if heart and mind truly repent. Boniface declared and then made it so.")

It is worth noting that simultaneous with the Jubilee bull, the pope issued another document stating that "many make themselves unworthy of such indulgences." He specifically identified "those false and wicked Christians who have brought or will bring forbidden goods to the Saracens," such as "Frederick, son of the late Peter, once king of the Aragonese, and the Sicilians, enemies to us and the Roman Church, and the Colonnas, condemned by us as rebels to the Apostolic See."

1350: The Doctrine of Indulgences

Upon the election of Clement V in 1305, the pope no longer resided in Rome, but in France. His successor, Clement VI, considering the unstable conditions in Rome at the time, did not deem it appropriate to return in person, but he decided nonetheless to celebrate a new Jubilee there in 1350. In his bull *Unigenitus Dei Filius* in 1343 written from Avignon, he declared, "Upon the advice of our brothers and in the fullness of apostolic power, we have decided to reduce the indulgence to the fiftieth year," taking into account the brevity of human life and referring to the biblical passage from Leviticus: "You shall declare the fiftieth year holy."

The basilica of St. John Lateran was added to the list of places to be visited, and the conditions for receiving indulgences remained as before. However, the pope clarified that "even those who, after starting their journeys to the basilicas, were legitimately prevented from reaching the city that year or died along the way or while in the city before completing the required number of days—if they were truly penitent and had confessed—would still receive the indulgence."

In this document, the pope provides the first formal explanation of the meaning of indulgences, describing them as "an infinite treasure for mankind, through which those who make use of it become participants in the friendship of God. [A treasure] distributed to the faithful through the blessed Peter, key-bearer of heaven, and his successors, his vicars on earth, and which is mercifully applied, for particular and reasonable causes, sometimes for a total, sometimes for a partial, remission of the temporal punishment due for sins."

Matteo Villani, a chronicler of this Jubilee, noted: "The throng of Christians going to Rome was impossible to number; but according to the estimate of those residing in the city, during Christmas and the solemn days following Lent until the holy Resurrection at Easter, there were continually in Rome twelve hundred thousand pilgrims; and then for the Ascension and Pentecost more than eight hundred thousand."

While Dante Alighieri likely attended the previous Jubilee, Francesco Petrarch was certainly present at this one. Petrarch described the abysmal state of the city, exacerbated by the devastating earthquake of September 1349: "The houses lie in ruins, the walls crumble, the temples are collapsing, the shrines are sinking into the ground, and the laws are trampled underfoot. The Lateran lies in ruins, the mother of all churches is roofless, exposed to the fury of wind and rain. The holy dwellings of St. Peter and St. Paul waver, and what was once the temple of the Apostles is now a formless heap of rubble that would move hearts of stone to pity."

1390: The Pope Returns to Rome

On January 17, 1377, Pope Gregory XI reestablished the Apostolic See in Rome. However, the social and religious situation he found there was dire, prompting his successor, Urban VI, to move the Jubilee forward to 1390 hoping to expedite the revitalization of the city.

Urban VI emphasized that "as human life becomes shorter and shorter, with many not even reaching their fiftieth year," and recalling that "in the thirty-third year of our Savior and Lord Jesus Christ, He paid the debt of Adam to the eternal Father and washed away the stain of original sin with His own blood," he proposed a new interval of 33 years between Jubilee celebrations.

He also completed the list of required visits to the four major basilicas by adding Santa Maria Maggiore, noting that "God Almighty performs many miracles in this church, as piously believed, through the intercession of the Blessed Virgin, and so it must be revered with all devotion."

After Urban's sudden death in October 1389, Pope Boniface IX oversaw the Jubilee, confirming his predecessor's decisions. However, he faced opposition from the first antipope of the Western Schism, Clement VII, who from his position in Avignon forbade his followers from traveling to Rome and issued a bull titled *Antiquus serpens* (Ancient Serpent), a derogatory reference to Boniface.

Despite the ban and the many compelled to adhere to it in their defection—particularly pilgrims from France and Spain—

Rome was still flooded with pilgrims from Germany, Hungary, Bohemia, Poland, and England. For those unable to make the pilgrimage—especially after a deadly outbreak of the plague around Pentecost—Boniface granted indulgences in their own regions, "provided they sent the offerings they would have brought themselves without delay to the [Roman] basilicas and churches." This led to the collection of approximately 100,000 gold florins, helping to replenish the depleted papal treasury.

1400: The Processions of the "Bianconi"

Although no bull of indiction has ever been found, the Jubilee of 1400 was celebrated under Pope Boniface IX at a time when Rome was embroiled in a fierce conflict between the powerful Colonna and Orsini families, with the pope himself living barricaded in his palace. (In fact, on January 15 of that year, he had to seek refuge in Castel Sant'Angelo to escape an attempted capture.)

This Holy Year was marked by the processions of penitents, mostly from France and northern Italy, who arrived in Rome dressed in white sackcloth and flagellated their bare backs while reciting litanies. These penitents, known as the "Bianconi" or "flagellants," were said to number over 120,000 in Rome at one point. Living in poor sanitary conditions and bad hygiene, they contributed to the spread of the plague, with nearly a thousand people dying per day.

Giovanni Sercambi from Lucca writes about these devotional acts in his *Chronicles*, describing "the moral decay of the world, filled with sin and violence, with peoples turning on one another and unable to stop the cycles of violence [...]. [I]t is the divine goodness that seeks to show a sign, so that the world might correct itself and come to a true understanding of God, so that everyone might abstain from sin and live virtuously." He vividly describes the penitents: "All walk with their clans, carrying Christ as their banner. [...] All cry out, 'Help us, God, peace, peace, merciful Lord.' [...] They beat their chests and backs, barefoot, naked, and they make restraints for their wretched bodies."

A letter dated 28 March 1400, sent from Rome to the merchant Francesco Datini in Prato, reports: "A door has been opened here at Saint John Lateran, which had not been opened for 50 years: passing through it three times grants forgiveness of both punishment and sin. It is a miracle, all the people passing through it. In the Jubilee ten years ago, that door was not opened because the pope did not allow it."

1423: Pilgrimages to the Catacombs

There is likewise no known bull of indiction for the Holy Year of 1423, but it can be assumed that Pope Martin V celebrated it following the precedent set by Urban VI, who had decreed an interval of only 33 years between Jubilees, in memory of the earthly life of Jesus. Ignoring the Jubilee of 1400, Martin referred to the one from 1390. On this occasion, he also canceled all local "jubilees" in response to the Council of Constance's insistence on limiting indulgences.

Martin, a native Roman, had been elected as the "one and only" pope in 1417 after the deposition of the three rival popes at the time—namely, John XXIII, Benedict XIII, and Gregory XII. He chose to return to live in Rome, which was still plagued by violence and epidemics. In preparation for the Jubilee, he organized a mission among the people in 1422, led by a great preacher and future saint, Bernardino of Siena.

Despite these challenges, there was a general atmosphere of spiritual renewal in Europe after the conclusion of the Great Schism, and numerous foreign pilgrims came to Rome. The writer Poggio Bracciolini describes the scene harshly, calling it "a flood of barbarians in Rome who filled the entire city with their filth and dirt." Indeed, many pilgrims died of the plague due to poor sanitary conditions.

The chronicler Nicola della Tuccia records that "Pope Martin later opened the Holy Door of Saint John [Lateran], and the pardons lasted for a year." In addition to the customary basilicas, the catacombs also became a pilgrimage destination, sparking a devotion that grew over time and led to the establishment of a papal commission for their oversight. The large underground areas of the Catacombs of Saint Sebastian were particularly popular. As noted by the English pilgrim John Capgrave, "If one does not stop in the chapels but continues straight, he will walk for the amount of time it takes to say the *Miserere mei Deus* four times."

1450: A Golden Door at St. Peter's

On 19 January 1449, with the bull *Immensa et innumerabilia*, Pope Nicholas V reinstated the original and more regular 50-year interval between Jubilees and offered a thoughtful reflection on God's mercy and gifts. He emphasized that his predecessors had chosen "certain times in which the rivers of divine mercy would flow more abundantly for the faithful people."

The Holy Year, celebrated from 24 December 1449 until Christmas of 1450, was called the "Golden Year," and some writers of the time described the opening of a "Golden Door" at St. Peter's Basilica, along with the other Holy Doors at St. John Lateran, Santa Maria Maggiore, and St. Paul Outside the Walls. The chronicler Giovanni Rucellai notes that "such was the devotion people had for the bricks and mortar that as soon as it was unsealed, in a rush people carried them away, and foreigners took them home as holy relics."

Many preachers, particularly Franciscans, were selected to hold missions for the people, explaining the doctrine of indulgences. They clarified the distinction between the remission of sins through the sacrament of reconciliation and the remission of temporal punishment connected to sins through the granting of indulgences obtained by fulfilling specific requirements. Special faculties were given to confessors to absolve even the gravest sins, normally reserved for bishops or canon penitentiaries.

Pilgrims from all over Europe flocked to Rome, greatly desiring to venerate the holy relics kept there. In the *Memoriale* of the Roman writer Paolo di Benedetto di Cola dello Mastro, it is recorded that "the pope ordered the Holy Face [the veil of Veronica] to be shown every Sunday [at St. Peter's] and the heads [of the Apostles Peter and Paul at the Lateran basilica] every Saturday; and all the relics of the churches in Rome were displayed, and the pope gave his blessing every Sunday at the hour of the blessing, in St. Peter's."

There was great celebration, especially for the canonization of Bernardino of Siena, which was celebrated by the pope on Pentecost. About 2,000 friars of the Franciscan order came to Rome, including three future saints: John of Capestrano (hero of the fight against the Turks), the great preacher James of the Marches, and the Spanish lay brother Diego d'Alcalá, tireless in his service to the sick.

1475: The Reduction to 25 Years

With the bull *Ineffabilis providentia* on 19 April 1470, Pope Paul II reconstructed the history of previous Jubilee arrangements and explained the reasons for the changes made by his predecessors, decreeing that, starting in 1475, Holy Years would be celebrated every 25 years.

His rationale was that "the span of human life is still very brief, and, pressed by our sins, frequent are the plagues and other mortal diseases, frequent are the severe persecutions by Turks and infidels against the faithful, and all of Christendom, fractured in past times, is still harassed by various, no less grievous, violences and subject to disastrous events and purges, while many other tribulations still persist among the peoples of Christ."

However, Pope Paul II died in July 1471, and it was his successor, Sixtus IV, who celebrated the Jubilee. In the bull *Quemadmodum operosi* of August 1473, he confirmed the previous decrees and extended all indulgences granted to churches, monasteries, and pious places for the duration of the Holy Year.

The invention of the printing press by Johannes Gutenberg, just about 20 years earlier, allowed for the wide dissemination of the Jubilee bull, indulgence handbooks, prayer books, and confession manuals. Of particular interest was the *Mirabilia urbis Romae*, a guidebook to the wonders of Rome that went on to have numerous updated editions.

At the end of 1475, a series of storms caused the Tiber River to overflow, spreading contagious diseases that discouraged many pilgrims from coming to Rome. As a result, the pope extended the Jubilee until Easter of 1476 and reduced the required visits to the basilicas for those coming from far away. He also granted some dioceses the possibility of acquiring the plenary indulgence by visiting four local churches.

1500: Indulgences for Souls in Purgatory

Pope Alexander VI, elected in August 1492, carefully prepared for the Jubilee marking the turn toward the second millennium. In the April 1498 bull *Consueverunt romani pontifices*, he emphasizes the spiritual character of the event, expressing the hope that "everyone would prepare his heart for the Lord, strive to improve his behavior, abstain from doing evil, and offer satisfaction to the Lord through penance, humility, the sacrifice of a contrite heart, and the simultaneous practice of almsgiving and pilgrimages."

The bull of indiction *Inter multiplices* was read from the Vatican *Loggia* on Holy Thursday of 1499, heralded by the sound of trumpets, in accordance with the Leviticus command: "On the Day of Atonement, you shall sound the horn throughout the land."

On 20 December 1499, the bull *Inter curas multiplices* outlined the conditions for obtaining the Jubilee indulgence: visiting the four major basilicas (once per day, for 30 days for Romans, 15 days for foreigners), confession, and communion (Vatican penitentiaries were allowed to absolve even the gravest sins). Additionally, the indulgence could be applied to souls in purgatory if pilgrims deposited "some alms for the restoration of the aforementioned Basilica of St. Peter into the designated collection box in St. Peter's Basilica."

Pope Alexander also decreed that, during Jubilee years, each of the four basilicas should have a designated Holy Door. The work on enlarging the portal at St. Peter's—kept open day and night throughout the Holy Year and guarded by four religious—led to the demolition of a beautiful medieval chapel decorated with mosaics and the relocation of the altar where the Veil of Veronica was kept. Due to a Tiber flood, the closing of the Holy Doors was postponed until Epiphany of 1501. The pope also commissioned Johannes Burckardt, a liturgist, to draft a ceremonial rite that, in part, is still used in Jubilee celebrations today.

1525: The First Jubilee Medal

The practice of requesting monetary offerings in exchange for granting indulgences, which had become common in the Vatican at that time, was one of the reasons that led Martin Luther to post his 95 theses on the door of the Wittenberg Cathedral in 1517, sparking the Protestant Reformation. The Jubilee of 1525 had to contend with this strong opposition, which argues: "The treasures of the Church from which the pope grants indulgences are not the merits of Christ and the saints," and, "Indulgences are 'pious fraud' imposed on the faithful."

Pope Leo X, with his decree *Postquam* of 1518, provides explanations concerning the meaning of indulgences, but it fell to his successor, Clement VII, to inaugurate and preside over this Jubilee, which also faced opposition from several Roman clerics, who were keen not to further provoke the Lutherans on the issue of indulgences and were concerned about the ongoing war between Charles V of Spain and Francis I of France.

On 17 December 1524, just a week before the traditional start date, Pope Clement issued the bull *Inter sollicitudines*, specifying that "on the vigil of the Nativity of Our Lord Jesus Christ, at the first vespers of said vigil, we will proceed to the basilica of the Blessed Peter and open with our own hands the door of this very same basilica, customarily opened for the greater devotion of the faithful during the Jubilee year." On this occasion, the pope minted the first commemorative Jubilee medal, featuring his own portrait on one side and the Holy Door on the other.

Despite Luther's strongly worded objections, which distinguished between Christ's Jubilee—granted freely to all through their faith—and the pope's Jubilee—which involved a pilgrimage to Rome and was seen as a lucrative superstition benefiting the Roman Curia—Clement established that for the indulgence to be applied to the souls of the deceased, their relatives would have to deposit "some alms into one of the chests set up in St. Peter's Basilica according to the order of our penitentiaries."

1550: The Holy Year Begins Late

The death of Pope Paul III on November 10, 1549, caused some turmoil regarding the Jubilee. His only initiative related to the event had been a decree earlier that year prohibiting "spikes in rent": "Whenever such a year occurs, for one year before and during said Holy Year or Jubilee, house rents may not be increased [...]. Furthermore, tenants cannot be evicted from rented houses unless the landlord truly needs it and swears the oath that he will occupy it himself for a year, under penalty of losing two years' rent if he falsely speaks."

It was therefore his successor, Julius III, who issued the bull *Si pastores ovium* on 24 February 1550, just two days after his enthronement on the Seat of Peter, retroactively marking the start of the Holy Year from Christmas 1549. On the same day, he opened the Holy Door of St. Peter's Basilica, which remained open until the Epiphany of 1551. These complications contributed to a low turnout of pilgrims, with only 50,000 reported to be in Rome during Easter. However, pilgrims were afforded better hospitality than in the past, thanks to the efforts of St. Philip Neri, the founder of the Oratory, who opened a hostel near the Ponte Sisto for poor and sick pilgrims, managed by the Confraternity of the Most Holy Trinity.

Michelangelo Buonarroti also participated in this Jubilee, who rode on horseback with his friend, the painter Giorgio Vasari, as they visited the seven churches of Rome. As a token of gratitude, the pope granted both of them a "double pardon," which may have inspired Michelangelo to write these verses to God: "Onde l'anima mia ancor si fida / di doppia aiuto nei miei doppi affanni" ["Thus my soul still trusts / In double aid for my double troubles"]. Another notable pilgrim was Ignatius of Loyola, founder of the Jesuits, who would be canonized in 1622 by Pope Gregory XV alongside Philip Neri and Teresa of Avila.

1575: The Jubilee of the Counter-Reformation

Twelve years after the close of the Council of Trent, which clarified and reinforced doctrinal and disciplinary unity within the Catholic Church (in response to the Protestant Reformation), Pope Gregory XIII used this Jubilee as an opportunity to accelerate the implementation of the Council's decrees across Christendom, summarized in the so-called "Tridentine Profession of Faith."

The decree on indulgences, approved at the Council of Trent on 4 December 1563, states: "The holy Synod teaches and commands that the use of indulgences, very beneficial for the Christian people, be preserved in the Church. [...] However, it desires that moderation be used in granting indulgences, to prevent excessive ease in granting them from weakening ecclesiastical discipline. [...] With this present decree, [the Synod] establishes the complete abolition of all unworthy financial transactions made to obtain them."

In the bull of proclamation *Dominus ac Redemptor noster*, issued on 10 May 1574, Pope Gregory XIII reaffirmed that Jesus Christ "left to the blessed Peter, prince of the Apostles, and to his successors, his vicars on earth, placed at the head of the holy Roman Catholic Church—which is the head, mother, and teacher of all others—full authority to remit sins, and further enriched the Church, his spouse, with the immense treasure of the merits of his own Passion (to which are added the merits of the most glorious ever Virgin Mary and all the saints), and entrusted this treasure to the said blessed Peter and his successors, so that with it the faithful might be helped in making satisfaction for the temporal penalties that often remain from the sins forgiven, thus making them more ready to receive the fruits of heavenly grace."

The socio-economic situation in Europe was still difficult. For this reason, the pope issued a special appeal to Maximilian II of Habsburg, Emperor of the Holy Roman Empire, and to all Christian kings and princes, urging them to "increase their merits before the Lord by supporting the piety of the pilgrims, and to be made participants in such a great and good work, by providing for the safety of the roads for the benefit of the pilgrims and by aiding the needy with charity and alms." The influx of pilgrims during the Holy Year was estimated to be around 400,000, while Rome at that time had a population of about 80,000 inhabitants.

1600: A Baroque Theater Jubilee

Rome became the "religious theater of the world," as "papal processions and those of noble families were united with the processions organized to visit the Roman basilicas." This is how historian Vittorino Grossi describes the Jubilee of 1600, which other scholars have termed "baroque," given that decorative and lavish theatrical elements predominated over the more traditional penitential themes.

The daily spectacle of faith and folklore, especially through the confraternities that had gained increasing prominence in previous Holy Years, reached its peak with the arrival of the "Band of Mercy" from Foligno: "By torchlight, they processed throughout the city, carrying representations of the mysteries of the passion, death, and resurrection of Christ. First came many children dressed as angels holding the instruments of the passion, followed by young women with their banners and a large group of boys holding olive branches. Then came Jesus, on a donkey, followed by the Apostles—all living figures representing their biblical characters and all the scenes of the passion," records a chronicle of the time.

In the bull of proclamation *Annus Domini placabilis*, dated 19 May 1599, Pope Clement VIII explicitly invites all bishops around the world to participate actively: "Brothers, bring the little ones with your word and example to the bosom of this most beloved mother who gave birth to them in Christ through the Gospel; bring the children to the father, the sheep to the supreme shepherd, the members to the head, the faithful to the rock of faith, upon which the entire structure of the Catholic Church is built."

The pope himself set the example by completing penitential visits to the basilicas sixty times, climbing the Holy Stairs on his knees, hearing numerous confessions, and personally serving twelve impoverished souls each day at the papal table. The cardinals, in turn, expressed their penitence by giving up their scarlet robes. Due to a severe attack of gout, Clement was only able to open the Holy Door of St. Peter's Basilica on December 31, and the closing ceremony was also delayed until January 13, 1601. An estimated three million pilgrims traveled to Rome for this Jubilee.

1625 Jubilee: The Visit to Santa Maria in Trastevere

To ward off the dangers of the plague that afflicted the Kingdom of the Two Sicilies, certain basilicas "outside the walls" were added for the first time as Jubilee destinations. Instead of San Paolo, the church of Santa Maria in Trastevere became a place of pilgrimage, while San Sebastiano and San Lorenzo were substituted with Santa Maria del Popolo and San Lorenzo in Lucina in the traditional itinerary of the seven churches.

In the bull of proclamation *Omnes gentes plaudite manibus*, dated 29 April 1624 (although published on August 6), Pope Urban VIII provides a rich biblical compendium to inspire spiritual and social renewal among the faithful. He particularly draws a parallel with the Jewish Jubilee, emphasizing that "back then, lost possessions fallen into the hands of others were recovered; now, through God's merciful grace, we reclaim the virtues, gifts, and merits which we have rightfully lost by sinning. Back then, exiles returned to their homeland; now the path to heaven is shown and opened to us, for we miserably wander in exile through this valley of tears."

Once again, bishops worldwide were invited to take up "the silver trumpets used in the Jubilee": "In order to receive heavenly gifts in this city, call the assembly, gather the people, sanctify the church, for we are strangers and pilgrims in this life, and here we have no lasting home, but seek the one to come."

Pope Urban VIII paid special attention to welcoming pilgrims, sponsoring various initiatives to establish hostels for the poor, and personally hosted bishops and foreign clergy in the

Vatican. He allocated two thousand gold *scudi* to the Confraternity of the Most Holy Trinity to ensure that it could continue its charitable works.

The pope was also highly effective in ensuring the safety of the streets of Rome. Through a specific edict, he forbade carrying weapons, stating that "it is most fitting that in this year of the Holy Jubilee, the city of Rome remains purged of all violence and iniquity." To prevent conflicts that had occurred in the past between some confraternities over processional privileges, the pope appointed officials to meet with the groups and ensure the orderly conduct of pilgrimages.

1650 Jubilee: The Call to the Tombs of the Apostles

In addition to the customary inspirations in the Jubilee bulls, Pope Innocent X, in *Appropinquat dilectissimi filii* (4 May 1649), makes special reference to Saints Peter and Paul, urging Christians to make the pilgrimage to Rome. He writes: "You are invited by the glorious remnants of the Apostles, held in such great veneration by all people from the very beginning of the newly born Church that those who came to them from distant parts of the world, even knowing that, with the persecutions of the emperors in effect, their worship would reveal them as Christians and put them at risk of death, still did not cease their sacred pilgrimages. Many, for this reason, were crowned with the palm of martyrdom."

The ongoing conflict between Spain and France moved Pope Urban VIII to issue a heartfelt appeal to Christian kings and their peoples: "You children of the promise, chosen race, people whom God has chosen for Himself, you who fear God, be you small or great, in one voice offer the sacrifice of praise in His temple, and in this year of remission and peace, forgive each other's offenses. Finally, laying down the arms that have long been mobilized in the disastrous shedding of Christian blood, come together with fraternal and joyful hearts in this mother to all believers, from whom you have all equally suckled the milk of faith."

The rivalry between France and Spain led the Spanish to assert their superiority by organizing lavish ceremonies, much to the displeasure of other confraternities. A chronicle from the time recounts that "the Spanish outdid themselves at dawn on Easter Sunday when they organized a grand procession in Piazza Navona, led by their national confraternity, that of the Resurrection. The square was transformed into a peristyle adorned with columns entwined in greenery and illuminated by 1,600 lamps. In the center stood choirs, while at both ends towered two great pavilions of the Castilians and Aragonese, one with the statue of the risen Christ and the other with that of His Mother. Those who took part in the procession said that this celebration alone was worth the pilgrimage from Spain to Rome."

1675 Jubilee: The Bull Read Twice

Drawing on an idea of his predecessor, Gregory XIII, Pope Clement X had the Jubilee bull *Ad apostolicae vocis oraculum,* dated 16 April 1674, read publicly on two occasions: on the Ascension (May 3), symbolizing the opening of the gates of heaven for repentant sinners, and on the Fourth Sunday of Advent (December 23), marking the death of the old liturgical year as it succumbs to the birth of the Holy Year.

The pope paid great attention to the spiritual dimension of the Jubilee, urging all bishops to instruct their faithful in "how to prepare themselves with contrite hearts and humble spirits, with persistent prayer and fasting, and with other works of piety to achieve the saving indulgences. Those who possess the wealth of this world should open their hearts and lift the poverty of their brothers; let them also be especially merciful to the pilgrims who come to Rome and, with great spiritual joy, renew and practice the holy hospitality so pleasing to God, which the early Christians cultivated even amidst the waves of persecution."

Despite being 84 years old, Pope Clement completed the required visits to the basilicas on foot five times, undeterred by the painful arthritis in his toe. With the support of cardinals and other Roman personages, he bolstered the works of hospitality shown to pilgrims. On Good Friday evening, he personally washed the feet of twelve pilgrims and then served dinner to 13,000 people. It is estimated that approximately 1.4 million people visited Rome during this Holy Year.

1700 Jubilee: A Jubilee for Two Popes

For the first and only time, the Holy Door was opened by one pope, Innocent XII, but closed by another, Clement XI. Pope Innocent XII passed away during the Holy Year on 27 September, and his successor was swiftly elected on November 23. Due to his poor health, Pope Innocent XII was unable to preside over the ceremony, and Cardinal Emmanuel Bouillon stood in for him.

In the bull of indiction *Regi saeculorum* on 18 May 1699, Pope Innocent XII expresses to his fellow bishops his heartfelt desire regarding Protestants: "If only we could welcome, together with you, in the same embrace of charity and fatherly love, those children who were once ours but are now fugitives from the Church. They were once close to us but have distanced themselves, cutting themselves off from the faith of their fathers and turning away from the bosom of their mother. We cannot dwell on this but in deep sorrow."

On 26 November, a violent flood of the Tiber River inundated much of Rome, causing transportation difficulties and problems for the Jubilee ceremonies. The Basilica of St. Paul, which became an island in the middle of a lake, was declared unusable and was temporarily replaced as a visitation spot, as had happened in 1625, by the Basilica of Santa Maria in Trastevere.

ᐟ These inconveniences, along with the fact that many pilgrims had not begun their journey during the *sede vacante*, prompted Pope Clement XI to decree that the plenary indulgence of the Holy Year would be granted to all faithful who attended the closing ceremony of one of the Holy Doors. The pope personally presided over the ceremony at St. Peter's, while three cardinal delegates were appointed to lead the ceremonies in the other three major basilicas. Two months later, on 25 February 1701, with the constitution *In supremo militantis ecclesiae*, Pope Clement extended the Jubilee's benefits to the entire Christian world.

1725: The Pope Relocates to the Vatican

Shortly after being elected pope, Benedict XIII issued the Jubilee bull *Redemptor et Dominus noster* on 26 June 1724, signaling his intent to personally embrace the spirituality of the Holy Year. To better preside over the ceremonies at St. Peter's Basilica, he moved his residence from the Quirinal Palace to the Vatican, allowing him to easily attend pilgrimages in other basilicas, visit the sick in hospitals, and comfort prisoners in jail.

On 29 May 1724, he made a powerful gesture during the Corpus Christi procession, walking on foot into St. Peter's Basilica and personally carrying the monstrance with the Blessed Sacrament, which was enormously inspiring to the faithful. To enhance pastoral care, he convened the Roman Provincial Council from 15 April to 29 May 1725 that culminated in a grand procession from St. John Lateran to Santa Croce in Gerusalemme.

His deep devotion to the Eucharist led him to grant a special indulgence: "To promote and increase the piety and devotion of the faithful toward the Most Holy and August Sacrament of the Body and Blood of Our Lord Jesus Christ, we grant, with said authority, to all Christian faithful outside the city who, having confessed and received Holy Communion, or at least truly repenting with the intent to confess, devoutly pray for howsoever much time one can during the Forty Hours' Devotion in the churches where it is held during this Jubilee Year, and every time one does so seven years and seven quarantines of imposed penances for each such act of devotion is conceded."

Amid the Jubilee celebrations, 370 former slaves of various nationalities arrived in Rome, liberated by the Mercedarians—founded in 1218 by St. Peter Nolasco to ransom Christian captives. After a procession to St. Peter's Basilica, Benedict XIII received them and gave each a medal with a plenary indulgence "at the moment of death" and a holy card depicting the Lamb of God.

1750: The First *Via Crucis* in the Colosseum

"Now that through the great mercy of God the war is over and peace between warring nations reigns, one hopes for the great voyage of foreigners and pilgrims of all nations to Rome." With these words in 1750 following the end of the war and the signing of the Peace of Aachen accord (18 October 1748), Pope Benedict XIV addressed the Italian bishops and urged them to provide the proper resources for an upright spiritual and liturgical life in their respective dioceses, such that "all those who come to Rome be not scandalized rather full of formation in what they have seen in Rome, certainly, but also in all the cities of the pontifical state."

The pope issued detailed instructions to bishops for preparing the faithful for the Jubilee indulgence (set forth in the encyclical *Apostolica constitutio* of 26 June 1749) and set guidelines for penitentiaries regarding confessions and absolutions (found in the lengthy apostolic letter *Convocatis* of 25 November 1749).

On 27 November 1750 in the moving shadow of the Colosseum (where many early Christians were martyred in Rome), Pope Benedict XIV approved the solemn observance of the *Via crucis* (Stations of the Cross). It was led by the Franciscan preacher

Leonardo da Porto Maurizio, who believed the devotion was a true and proper pilgrimage, or in his own words, a "stairway to heaven." At the same time, various missions for the people were held throughout the city by Jesuit, Dominican, and Servite preachers. At the conclusion of the Holy Year, the pope expressed great satisfaction with its success and extended the Jubilee indulgence to the entire Christian world: "If one is truly penitent, frequents confession and communion, within six months from the day this letter is promulgated in each diocese, if the cathedral of one's diocese is visited or those churches most important, and another three churches of the same region at least once per day for fifteen days consecutive or at intervals [...] and where one offers devout prayer to God [...] we concede and mercifully in the Lord extend a plenary indulgence, pardon and remission of all one's sins, as if one had visited the four basilicas or churches we have formally designated."

1775: Another Delayed Jubilee

In 1775, the Holy Year was delayed due to the death of Pope Clement XIV, who had proclaimed it in the bull *Salutis nostrae auctor* on 30 April 1774. The Jubilee was opened on 26 February 1775 by his successor Pope Pius VI, elected just ten days earlier. The bull reaffirmed the customary provisions of previous Jubilees.

On the same day that he closed the Holy Door of St. Peter's, Pius VI extended the Jubilee to the entire Catholic world and promulgated his encyclical *Inscrutabile divinae sapientiae*. Here in great clarity he presents the challenges of the time: "New ideas are infiltrating places of higher education, noble houses, royal palaces, and, it is horrible to say, found even within the sacristy. [...] The world leaders either do not recognize the danger posed by arreligious philosophy in their regard and the public order, or they do not possess the courage to confront it. [...] Revolution even in the realm of the political is inevitable when the existence of God or his providence is denied."

Pope Pius VI was later taken prisoner by Napoleon's French army in February 1798 and died in exile on 29 August 1799 at Fort Valence. His successor, Pope Pius VII who was elected on 14 March 1800, did not declare a Jubilee but issued a document on 24 May 1800 granting a plenary indulgence to the faithful under specific conditions. These included "visiting designated churches at least once with proper interior devotion and outward manner, or at least some of the churches indicated by the local Ordinaries; and there pray for an appropriate amount of time for the triumph of the Holy Mother Catholic Church, an end to heresy, and peace and accord among all Christian realms; fasting on Wednesday, Friday, and Saturday of one or other of the periods mentioned in precedence, devoutly receiving the Eucharist on the first Sunday after this week, or another day of the same week; and giving alms to the poor as one is compelled to do in his devotion."

1825: Condemnation of Secret Societies

In 1825, the socio-political climate following the 1815 Congress of Vienna was all but peaceful, yet Pope Leo XII (elected in 1823) decided to proceed with the Holy Year. On 24 May 1824, he issued the bull *Quod hoc ineunte*, which was read aloud at the four major basilicas of Rome by apostolic delegates accompanied by tambourine players on foot and trumpet players on horseback. (Although due to a fire at St. Paul Outside the Walls, Santa Maria in Trastevere was once again substituted as one of the pilgrimage sites.)

In this document, the pope explains that "at the opening of this century because of the mortal challenges of these times much was we lament omitted, but we now at last turn to the Lord and his ready mercy, and it has been granted upon our humility to joyfully announce that this mercy is at hand." During this Holy Year (which was here referenced as "omitted") on 13 March 1825, Leo XII addressed the growing unrest in society, strongly reaffirming his condemnation of secret societies, stating that "no clandestine sects should think they are excluded from our apostolic judgment, nor use this as an excuse to deceive the unwary or uninformed. [...] We prohibit in perpetuity all societies of the occult (whatever their names or titles may be), as much those now in existence as those that follow or propose to act in such ways as these against the Church and reigning civil powers."

Pope Leo XII himself participated in many Jubilee devotions, including a barefoot pilgrimage to the basilicas. On one occasion, he led a penitential procession of the College of Cardinals to Santa Maria Maggiore, St. John Lateran, Santa Maria in Trastevere, and finally to St. Peter's Basilica, where they sang a *Te Deum* in thanksgiving.

Following the disruption of the 1800 Holy Year, the Jubilee of 1850 was also not celebrated in its usual form, as Pope Pius IX was exiled in Gaeta on 24 November 1848 due to the unrest that preceded the proclamation of the Roman Republic. Instead, a document signed by Cardinal Costantino Patrizi Naro, the pope's vicar, granted a plenary indulgence "in the form of a Jubilee" to the faithful who, between June 19 and July 9, confessed, received communion, and participated in the novena of Saints Peter and Paul, or attended specific events of formation and reflection in certain Roman churches.

1875: The Holy Year of the "Prisoner Pope"

In 1875, Pope Pius IX, now a self-declared "prisoner" in the Vatican after the "breach of Porta Pia" (20 September 1870) and the annexation of Rome by the Kingdom of Italy (and the plebiscite the following 2 October), still chose to celebrate the Holy Year. He issued the bull *Gravibus Ecclesiae et hujus saeculi calamitatibus* on 24 December 1874.

In this document he recalls that it had been impossible to celebrate the 1850 Jubilee due to the "sorrowful circumstances of the times." He adds, "But these grave circumstances that now impede us from opening the Jubilee are rather than abating instead, God so allowing it, increasing daily. Nevertheless, in consideration of so many evils that afflict the Church, the effort to tear her down and extinguish all faith in Christ, corrupt her sound doctrine and propagate the poison of impiety, [...] we are of the mind that we ought not allow that in this atmosphere the Christian people be deprived of this soothing benefit."

Due to the difficult situation, the traditional methods of obtaining an indulgence were modified. Faithful were to be "truly repentant, confessed, and communicated," and then devoutly visit the designated basilicas daily for fifteen days. In Rome, these were the basilicas of Saints Peter and Paul, St. John Lateran, and Santa Maria Maggiore. Outside of Rome, pilgrims were to visit "their cathedrals or main churches, and three other churches of one's town or city or region designated as such churches as decreed by the respective local Ordinary."

The Holy Year was inaugurated on 11 February 1875 at St. Peter's Basilica without the opening of the Holy Door, in the presence only of the clergy from the Diocese of Rome. The processions were subdued, and few pilgrim groups arrived, primarily from France and Germany, and more as a sign of support for the pope than to visit as traditional Jubilee pilgrims.

1900: The Work of the International Committee

In 1900, Pope Leo XIII, who had been 14 years old during the last solemn Jubilee in 1825, reflected on his vivid memories of that time in the bull of indiction for the Holy Year of 1900. He recounted seeing "the flow of pilgrims, the multitude orderly gathered around the most august temples, apostolic men delivering public sermons, the most renowned places resounding with divine praises, and the pope, accompanied by cardinals, in front of everyone offering examples of piety and charity."

In the spirit of ensuring that "everywhere on earth, people might understand the reverence owed to Jesus Christ the Savior during this fleeting time," he issued the bull *Properante ad exitum* on 11 May 1899 to announce the Jubilee. Then, on 25 May, he published the encyclical *Annum sacrum*, through this consecrating humanity to the Sacred Heart of Jesus in preparation for the Holy Year of 1900. An international committee, led by Count Giovanni Acquaderni (co-founder of Catholic Action), was tasked with organizing the Jubilee, as he had already been promoting devotion to Christ the Redeemer for many years.

On 24 December, the Holy Door of St. Peter's was opened in a solemn ceremony accompanied by the Vatican basilica choir, directed by maestro Lorenzo Perosi. Perhaps even more meaningful were the midnight Masses held on 31 December and 1 January 1899–1900, which Pope Leo XIII ordered to be celebrated in all churches worldwide, with the exposition of the Blessed Sacrament.

The development of the railway system allowed pilgrims to reach Rome by train, and Italy's railway network had expanded over 10,000 kilometers. Despite this, the political tensions of the time, including the unresolved bad relations between Italy and the Vatican (although the signed accords were not far off) and the assassination of King Umberto I of Savoy on 29 July limited the number of pilgrims to around half a million.

1925: The Pope's Intention for Peace

In 1925, following the devastation of World War I, Pope Pius XI expresses his intentions in the bull *Infinita Dei misericordia*, issued on 29 May 1924, wherein he indicates that his primary intention for himself and all the faithful is to pray for "peace, not merely written in treaties, but alive in the hearts of people, peace that must be restored among nations, which even if today this seems closer than it has in the past, is still farther away than our shared expectations would want [...]"; and pray "that all non Catholics enter the true Church of Christ"; and "that finally the situation in Palestine is brought to order, such as the holy rights due Catholics requires."

To visibly demonstrate the catholicity, or universality, of the Church, Pius XI established a missionary exhibit at the Lateran complex. During the grand opening on 21 December 1924, he stated, "We have desired it for the honor of our Lord Jesus Christ [...] for the honor of the holy Roman Church [...] and we wanted this missionary exposition because we desire blessings from this magnificent occasion of the Holy Year, the Jubilee that will gather around our fatherly heart many of our good children from all parts of the world."

For the first time pilgrims arrived in Rome by air, with the first groups coming in from Argentina and Uruguay on 22 December. Chronicles from the time also mention the "grand display of electricity" used to illuminate the city, with thousands of lamps and spotlights glowing from St. Peter's dome and other landmarks resplendent at night.

To conclude the Holy Year, Pope Pius XI renewed the consecration of humanity to the Sacred Heart of Jesus and instituted the solemn Feast of Christ the King of the Universe. Responding to objections that "Christ's regal dignity is already honored in other feasts," he explained that "whereas the material object of the current feasts of Our Lord is Christ Himself, the formal object in them is entirely distinct from the name of Christ's royal authority."

1933–34: An Extraordinary Holy Year

For the first time in the history of the Catholic Church, Pope Pius XI declared an extraordinary Jubilee to commemorate "the completion of the redemption of humanity," marking 1,900 years since the death and resurrection of Jesus Christ. The pope clarifies, "Although it is not entirely certain in terms of historical accuracy which year it should be dated to, the event, or rather the order of miraculous things accomplished, is of such great magnitude and importance that it would be inappropriate to let it pass in silence."

The Holy Door of St. Peter's Basilica was personally opened by Pope Pius XI on 2 April 1933, Passion Sunday, and was closed by him as well on 2 April 1934, which was Easter Monday. The faithful response exceeded expectations, with the number of pilgrims in the first six months already surpassing the total number of visitors to Rome during the Jubilee of 1925. Pilgrims came from distant places, including Alaska, Chile, New Zealand, and China. Pope Pius XI was tireless, holding about 650 audiences and delivering an equal number of speeches and addresses. Among the canonized saints that year were John Bosco, founder of the Salesians, and Bernadette Soubirous, the visionary of Lourdes.

In addition to the usual requirements of confession, communion, and three visits to the four major papal basilicas, Pius XI requested that the prayers of the faithful focus "on the memory of the divine redemption, particularly the Passion of the Lord." He asked that "prayers be recited five times before the Blessed Sacrament, that the Our Father, Hail Mary, and Glory be, once again be said for the pope's intentions; that all might three times recite before the image of a crucifix the Creed and one time the hymn, 'We adore You, Oh Christ, and we bless You,' or some other similar verse; that one place himself before the *Vergine Deipara* [Blessed Virgin, Mother of God] and there seven times in honor of her sorrow recite the angelic Ave Maria adding one time the prayer '*Santa Madre, deh, voi fate,*' or a some other similar prayer; and lastly, that one approach the holy altar of confession and devoutly profess once again the Catholic faith in its official formulation."

1950: The Jubilee of the Dogma of the Assumption

Pope Pius XII called the 1950 Jubilee "The Year of the Great Comeback and Great Forgiveness," and offered a perpetual indulgence to anyone who recited the prayer he composed for the Holy Year once a month. He made it easier for the faithful to gain the Jubilee indulgence by reducing the number of required visits to the four major basilicas to just one, in each of which they were to recite the Our Father, Hail Mary, and Glory be three times, plus once more for the intentions of the pope, along with the Creed.

In the bull *Iubilaeum maximum*, issued on 26 May 1949, Pius XII outlines his intentions for this holy year, particularly praying for "the long-desired peace in the hearts of all, in familial relationships, in individual nations, and in the universal community of peoples." He expressed hope, shortly after the end of World War II, that "those who are refugees, those who are prisoners, those who wander far from their origins may soon return to their beloved homelands."

In his Christmas radio message *Non mai forse* on 23 December 1949, the pope further elaborates the spiritual importance of this Holy Year as "crucial for the hoped-for religious renewal of the modern world, and decisive for the spiritual crisis gripping the souls of our time. The longed-for harmonization of heavenly and earthly values, the task and duty of our generation, will come to pass, or at least be expedited, if the faithful remain steadfast in their resolutions and tenacious in their undertakings, and do not allow themselves to be seduced by vain utopias or swayed by selfish interests."

The most significant day of the Jubilee was 1 November 1950, when Pius XII proclaimed the dogma of the Assumption of the Blessed Virgin Mary into Heaven. Over a million faithful were present for the ceremony, during which the pope consecrated the Church and humanity to the Immaculate Heart of Mary. During the closing celebration of the Holy Door, Pope Pius XII also announced the discovery of the tomb of St. Peter, the "Prince of the Apostles," directly beneath the dome of St. Peter's Basilica.

1975: Renewal After the Council

A decade after the close of Vatican II, Pope Paul VI decided to celebrate another Jubilee Year. In his address on 9 May 1973 announcing the decision, he confessed to questioning "whether such a tradition is worthy of being maintained in our time, so different from the past, and so influenced, on one hand, by the religious spirit impressed on ecclesial life by the recent Council, and, on the other hand, by the practical disinterest of much of the modern world toward rituals of past centuries. We are immediately convinced that the celebration of the Jubilee Year not only fits within the coherent spiritual line of the Council, which we are committed to faithfully carrying out, but can also correspond and contribute to the Church's tireless and loving efforts to meet the moral needs of our time and to interpret its deep aspirations."

The themes of the Jubilee were the renewal of humanity and reconciliation with God. Unlike previous jubilees, it began on 10 June 1973, the solemnity of Pentecost, in local churches worldwide, "such that the whole Church scattered across the earth might immediately begin to enjoy this great occasion [...] and better prepare for the culminating and concluding moment that will be celebrated in Rome in 1975."

Paul VI encouraged the faithful to engage in specific acts of charity and faith, "serving our brothers in need, in Rome and in churches worldwide. These works do not need to be grand, although they are not discouraged; in many cases, smaller initiatives, as we say today, will suffice, in the spirit of evangelical charity."

An estimated ten million pilgrims came to Rome, but radio and television broadcasts allowed even more people to participate in key events. For the closing of the Holy Door alone, an audience of 350 million listeners tuned in, and Paul VI granted the Apostolic Blessing and plenary indulgence live on air.

1983–84: The Jubilee of Redemption

Although Pope Pius XI had scheduled the next Jubilee for 2033 at the conclusion of the 1933 Holy Year, Pope John Paul II wanted to renew the idea and celebrate another Jubilee of Redemption in 1983–84, marking 1,950 years since the death and resurrection of Jesus Christ. The announcement of this Jubilee surprised even the cardinals, who were gathered for a consistory on 26 November 1982. In the bull *Aperite portas Redemptori*, issued on 6 January 1983, the pope echoes the appeal he made at the start of his pontificate: "Open the doors to the Redeemer [...] to His Paschal mystery, the pinnacle of divine revelation and the supreme act of God's mercy toward humanity in every age."

The Holy Door of St. Peter's Basilica was opened on 25 March 1983, the Feast of the Annunciation, following a penitential procession from the one of Rome's most ancient churches, Santo Stefano degli Abissini. Symbolically, John Paul II used the pastoral staff and hammer that Pius XI had used in the 1933 Jubilee. His prayer was that this Holy Year might "become a call to the contemporary world, which sees justice and peace on the horizon of its desires, yet continues to make room for sin, and lives amid growing tensions and threats, and seems to be heading in a dangerous direction."

On that solemn day, it was also publicly announced that Umberto II of Savoy, the last King of Italy who had died just a week prior, had donated the Shroud of Turin (upon which is the impressed figure of Christ) to the pope. John Paul II prayed to the Savior at the closing ceremony of the Holy Door on 22 April 1984, Easter Sunday: "Christ yesterday and today, the beginning and the end: What He opens no one can shut; What He shuts, no one can open. To Him be glory and power for all ages."

2000: The Jubilee of the Third Millennium

The grand Jubilee that marked the beginning of the Third Millennium was carefully prepared by Pope John Paul II, starting with the Jubilee of Redemption and an extended Marian Year (7 June 1987–15 August 1988). Then, in his apostolic letter *Tertio millennio adveniente*, issued on 10 November 1994, he invited all the faithful to a three-year period of preparation focusing on Jesus Christ (1997), the Holy Spirit (1998), and God the Father (1999), without missing an opportunity to offer another consecration to Mary.

In the bull *Incarnationis mysterium*, issued on 29 November 1998, the pope calls out to everyone: "Let no one exclude himself from the Father's embrace in this Jubilee year. The joy of forgiveness must be stronger and greater than any resentment. In doing so, the Bride will shine before the eyes of the world with that beauty and holiness that come from the Lord's grace. [...] Therefore, let our gaze be fixed on the future. The merciful Father does not count our sins if we have truly repented. Now He is doing something new, and in His forgiving love, He anticipates the new heavens and the new earth. Let faith be renewed, hope grow, and charity become ever more active, in view of a renewed commitment to Christian witness in the world of the next millennium."

The requirements for obtaining the Jubilee indulgence included, in addition to the usual confession, communion, and prayer for the pope's intentions, the following items: a pilgrimage to a shrine or Jubilee site, participation in Mass or a pious exercise, visiting and spending time with those in need, contributing to religious or social causes, dedicating time to community service, abstaining from non-essential consumption (such as smoking or alcohol) for at least a day, fasting, abstinence from meat, or making an appropriate donation to the poor.

The special occasion of the turn of the millennium and the remembrance of the 2000th anniversary of Christ's birth inspired a rich program with numerous events for various groups of the faithful. Some of the most heart-moving moments included an ecumenical service at St. Paul Outside the Walls attended by 22 leaders of Christian denominations, a *mea culpa* ceremony in St. Peter's Square to ask forgiveness for the sins committed by members of the Church, a commemoration of 20th century martyrs in the Colosseum, and World Youth Day at Tor Vergata, which drew around two million young people.

2015–2016: The First "Thematic" Jubilee

Unlike previous Jubilee years—which were traditionally associated with anniversaries of the birth or death of Jesus—the Jubilee of Mercy initiated by Pope Francis was celebrated from 8 December 2015 (the Feast of the Immaculate Conception) until 20 November 2016 (the Feast of Christ the King). This Jubilee was uniquely tied to the theme of God's mercy.

The theme was confirmed by the title of the bull of indiction, *Misericordiae vultus*, which begins by explaining that "Jesus Christ is the face of the Father's mercy." The pope elaborates that the Father, "rich in mercy," revealed His name to Moses as "merciful and gracious" and continuously makes His divine nature known throughout history, and finally sends His Son, "born of the Virgin Mary, to reveal His love to us in a definitive way." The unusual choice of dates for the opening and closing (traditionally set around Christmas) highlighted the inseparable relationship between the Redeemer and His Mother.

A unique aspect of the Jubilee of Mercy was the simultaneous opening of a "Door of Mercy" in cathedrals in every diocese across the world alongside the Holy Door of the Roman cathedral of St. John Lateran. This was done to visibly manifest the global communion of the Church during the celebration, a "visible sign of communion among the whole Church." In fact, Pope Francis personally opened a Holy Door at the cathedral in Bangui, Central African Republic, on 29 November 2015, an unprecedented gesture during his pastoral visit to the country. Another notable feature was the establishment of the "Missionaries of Mercy"—priests granted the authority to forgive sins typically reserved for the Apostolic See or diocesan bishops, such as the desecration of the Eucharist or abortion. This was meant as a "sign of the Church's maternal care for God's people, helping them to delve deeply into the richness of this mystery, so central to the faith."

Key events of that Holy Year included the introduction of a Jubilee day for prisoners, a vigil titled "Drying the Tears" for those in great need of consolation, and a series of "Jubilee Signs," where Pope Francis personally visited places of suffering, poverty, and marginalization as a witness to the works of mercy. One of the most powerful symbols was the opening of the "Holy Door of Charity" at the diocesan Caritas shelter on Via Marsala in Rome, which further emphasized the pope's concern for the poor and vulnerable. From 8–14 February 2016, the relics of two Capuchin saints, Padre Pio of Pietrelcina and Leopold Mandic, were displayed in St. Peter's Basilica, highlighting their exemplary roles as tireless, welcoming, and patient confessors during this Holy Year dedicated to mercy.

For more resources helpful to English-speaking pilgrims, please visit the following websites:

The Pontifical North American College:
https://www.pnac.org

The Canadian Pontifical College:
https://www.generalsaintsulpice.org/en/

The Venerable English College:
https://www.vecrome.org

The Pontifical Scots College:
https://www.scotscollege.org

The Pontificio Collegio Filippino:
https://pcfroma.org

The Pontifical Irish College:
https://www.irishcollege.org